More Praise For
Latina Power

"Very empowering! Dr. Nogales reveals our need to acknowledge, awaken, and utilize the inner power and strengths we already possess in order to take control of our lives and succeed."

—Jacqueline Obradors, actress
(*NYPD Blue, Tortilla Soup*)

"Like my mother used to say, 'Educate a man and you will educate his sons; educate a woman, and you will educate generations.' Dr. Nogales' book shows Latinas that we have the power to do precisely that. It sends the vital message that we must value who we are, and use our strengths to get on with the business of developing our full potential."

—Lupe Ontiveros, actress, *Real Women Have Curves*

"*Latina Power* engages the Latina Soul into a journey of self-discovery, sisterhood, and self-love. It calls upon all Latinas to unite, giving each other a safe place for their true selves to come alive. What a beautiful feeling!"

—Yasmin Davidds-Garrido, author, *Empowering Latinas:
Breaking Boundaries, Freeing Lives*

"Quite simply *Latina Power* is a terrific book that should be read by Latinas in all walks of life. Not only does Dr. Nogales give Latinas a great gift by identifying and acknowledging the strengths inherent in our culture and women, she turns negative stereotypes upside down and provides the reader with a practical roadmap for self-empowerment and personal accomplishment. Best of all *Latina Power* reminds women that you can create the life you want for yourself. Bravo!"

—Yolanda Nava, author, *It's All in the Frijoles*

"Ana Nogales creatively presents culturally consonant strategies of empowerment for Latinas. Her inspirational case studies arouse a resounding sense of 'Si se puede!' "
—Carola Suárez-Orozco, Ph.D., Executive Director, David Rockefeller Center for Latin American Studies

"Latinas are finally able to find our reflection in this book, which provides an invaluable guide to strengthening cultural attributes toward self-fulfillment and success. Latina Power is a pioneering work essential for understanding the largest group of contemporary culture bearers and transformers: Latinas."
—Dr. Carmen Carrillo, President and CEO, California Women's Commission on Addictions

"Latinas of all ages will cheer for *Latina Power* as they recognize themselves—their strengths, their struggles, and their potential for success—in its inspiring pages."
—Martha Samano, President, ALLA, Alliance for Latino Leaders in Action

"*Latina Power* will be especially inspiring for Latinas seeking their voice and wishing to embrace their power. It's a user-friendly tool that validates our totality."
—Gloria Barajas, former National President, MANA

"Latina Power tells the story of the Hispanic woman in the United States, her cultural identity, and the positive and negative stereotypes she confronts in a society where the past denotes a culture much different from the one she lives today. Ana Nogales and Laura Golden Bellotti reveal seven elements for a positive attitude to practice a healthier personal and professional life."
—*Semana,* Houston, TX

**Using 7 Strengths You Already Have
to Create the Success You Deserve**

LATINA POWER!

DR. ANA NOGALES

with Laura Golden Bellotti

A Fireside Book
Published by Simon & Schuster
New York   London   Toronto   Sydney   Singapore

To my mother

You were my guiding force, inspiring me toward a better life. My gratitude and unending love will always light my way.

FIRESIDE
Rockefeller Center
1230 Avenue of the Americas
New York, NY 10020

FIRESIDE and colophon are registered trademarks of Simon & Schuster, Inc.

For information about special discounts for bulk purchases,
please contact Simon & Schuster Special Sales: 1-800-456-6798
or business@simonandschuster.com

Designed by Ruth Lee

Manufactured in the United States of America

1 3 5 7 9 10 8 6 4 2

Library of Congress Cataloging-in-Publication Data is available

ISBN 0-7432-3630-0

Contents

Las Mujeres

Espíritu Creativo

Elena Avila: Curandera and Registered Nurse
Julz Chávez: Creator and Co-Founder, Get Real Girl, Inc.
Leticia Herrera: Chairman, Extra Clean, Inc.
Anita Pérez Ferguson: Author and Political Skills Trainer
Martha Montoya: Cartoonist
Silvia Bolaños: National Sales Director, Yves Rocher Cosmetics

The *Aguantadoras*

Esperanza Martínez: Artist
Dr. Estela Martínez: Anesthesiologist
Mercedes Sosa: Singer
Dr. Mary López: Professor of Endocrinology

The *Comadres*

Linda Gutiérrez: Chair, National Hispana Leadership Institute
Isabel Allende: Writer
María Hinojosa: TV and Radio Journalist

The *Diplomáticas*

María Pérez-Brown: TV Producer
Dr. Antonia Pantoja: Social Activist

Loretta Sánchez: U.S. Congresswoman
Linda Sánchez: U.S. Congresswoman
María Macías: Teacher
Lisa Fernández: Olympic Gold Medal Softball Player; Assistant Coach,
   UCLA Bruins Softball Team

The *Atrevidas*

Sor Juana Inés de la Cruz: Writer and Poet
Dr. Sandra Milán: Medical Researcher
Nely Galán: Entertainment Executive
Dr. Elvia Niebla: National Coordinator of Global Change Research for
   the U.S. Forest Service
Olga Marta Peña Doria: Professor of Theater

The *Malabaristas*

María Elena Salinas: Co-Anchor, Univision National News
Dr. Leticia Márquez-Magaña: Biology Professor
Dr. Eleonora Goldberg: Molecular Biologist
Elizabeth Pena: Actress
Silvia Piñal: Actress
Liz Torres: Comedienne

Las Reinas

Eva de la O: Opera Singer and Director, Musica de Camara, Inc.
Fern Espino: Business Executive
Cristina Saralegui: TV Host and Journalist
Linda Alvarado: President and CEO, Alvarado Construction, Inc.; Owner,
   Colorado Rockies Baseball Franchise
Norma Aleandro: Actress

Sharing Their Power

Sonia Marie De León de Vega: Music Director and Conductor, Santa
   Cecilia Orchestra; Music Educator
Hilda Solís: U.S. Congresswoman
Christy Haubegger: Founder, *Latina* Magazine
Jaci Velásquez: Singer/Songwriter
Angélica María: Actress and Singer

1

The 7 Latina Power Strengths

When I was about seven years old, I played almost every day with my next door neighbor, Miguelito. In fact, we had so much fun together that we promised each other we would get married when we grew up. One day, as we were building our "tent house" out of blankets and dining room chairs, my mother and my great-aunt, Tía Rosa, called me over. They had heard Miguelito and me talking about our future marriage, and they said to me, "Ani, when you grow up, you must look for a man to marry who has enough money, so that you'll have a good future for yourself." I remember feeling disgusted with what they said. And I very spontaneously answered back, "You don't have to worry about that, because I will be the one making the money." That brief conversation stayed in my mind always—and since then I have told myself that I would never look for *pesos* in a man. I would choose a husband based on other things—because I would make the money myself. I was right—and I did.

I think that the kind of passionate and focused determination I had then—and still have—is inherent in all Latinas. The challenge is to recognize such qualities in ourselves and to use them to get where we want to go in life. As Latinas, we always have succeeded in holding our families together, managing relationships, raising our children, surviving crises, making our pennies count. Now these abilities can help us qualify for the careers we envision and for the bigger job of creating a better society.

The idea for *Latina Power* came to me over a period of years, as I noticed how many creative, determined, courageous Latinas had overcome various obstacles to fulfill their dreams and make a difference in the world. And it struck me that, contrary to what many people think about Latino culture holding women back, the reasons for these women's successes lay in the very qualities which have their roots in our cultural origins. As I began to look more closely at the success stories of Latinas from all walks of life, I identified seven core Latina Power Strengths that we develop as a result of being born into a Latino family and/or growing up in a Latino community. In this chapter we're going to explore these qualities, and then you'll have a chance to identify which of them are most strongly apparent in your own life by taking a self-evaluation test at the end of the chapter. As the book unfolds you'll learn how to capitalize on each of these seven qualities as you hear from successful Latinas who have enriched their lives and the lives of those around them by doing just that.

Perhaps the quality that stands out in your mind, the one that was emphasized the most to girls in your family, is to be "giving." I know that in most Latino families women are taught to be giving—to your husband, to your children, to other people's children, to your extended family, to your community. And in Latino families everywhere, girls continue to learn from their mothers and grandmothers, who embody *la sufrida y abnegada,* that it is a woman's responsibility to give their lives totally to the welfare of their children and family. For some of our *abuelas y mamis* the challenge was especially great, because they had many children and had to work outside the home to support them, in addition to doing all the housework and child care. Often our mothers or aunts or grandmothers worked from sunrise until late at night in order to get it all done. And they did all of this with *orgullo de sí mismas*.

That sense of female devotion and sacrifice is ingrained in us, but we may feel ambivalent about it—both appreciating and resenting it at the same time. We wonder if there isn't a way of life—beyond what the older women in our families experienced—that could bring us more personal fulfillment. What I hope you'll discover by reading this book is the powerful untapped side to that "givingness" that we inherit from our Latino culture: our capacity to give to and nourish ourselves. Having learned so well how to be giving, we can now give some of that attention, love, sacrifice, and devotion to ourselves. We can be as giving to ourselves as we are to others, and in doing so we can accomplish great things. We can not only feel more fulfilled in our lives and make a contribution to the world outside our families, but we can be role models to our children so that they'll know *they* can go out and accomplish great things for themselves too.

Surpassing Family Expectations
A Bit of Personal History

Neither of my parents had a high school education. My father's priority was to work when he was a teenager, because making money to survive was more important than going to school. My mother was an excellent student, but when she was fifteen her father died and she had to drop out of school in order to work and support herself and her family. So even though my parents understood the value of higher education, neither of them had personally experienced the benefits of it.

Although my mother always wanted me to marry and have children, she believed that a woman should not depend on a man completely. One reason she gave was that some men can be abusive, so she believed that it is always good to have your own career in case the marriage doesn't last. Another reason was unspoken: She once had envisioned a career for herself, but due to the financial strain on her family after her father passed away, she couldn't pursue it. So she placed those expectations—and those dreams—on me. She thought I was smart and that I should go for it. And yet, at the same time, given the practical world and culture in which we lived, my mom wanted me to know how to cook, clean house, knit, sew, wash clothes, and raise children—because I would need those skills when I got married. So both messages were there in her dealings with me.

As a preteen and teenager I absolutely hated having to do household chores, but I excelled in math and science. My parents were very concerned, because they believed a woman needed to have those domestic skills in order to be a good housewife. What would my destiny be? they worried. My father decided that I should learn a marketable skill, in case misfortune should strike and I couldn't find a husband. Actually, that concern probably stemmed from the fact that I was very rebellious, so my parents were worried that no man would be able to tolerate this in me. I wasn't the typical *niña obediente* who did all her housework and would fit easily into the homemaker role. So when I was a teenager my dad took me to meet a friend of his who owned a beauty school in Buenos Aires and enrolled me in it. I hated it, and after about three months I dropped out. Again my parents worried, "What is she going to do with her future?" With my father's prominent example foremost in my mind—he had done well in business without a formal education—I told myself at the age of fifteen that I didn't need to finish school: "Why have all this stress in my life when I can be successful without a high school diploma?"

I set out to prove to my parents—and to myself—that I didn't need an education. Having learned how to type, I started looking for a job. I went on a couple of interviews, and finally someone called back wanting to hire me. He told me that, even though my office skills weren't that sharp, I could work for him. There was a catch, though. I would not only have to do office work, I would be expected to do "private work" for him as well—the implication being that I would have to perform certain unsavory favors for him. That was an eye-opener for me!

This man confirmed the warning my mother had given me about abusive men. So now I was even more convinced that I needed to be independent, that I needed to rely only on myself. At that point I decided that I was going to finish high school and get a college education so that I could get a job where *I* would be the one in power. A job I would not only enjoy but one in which no one could ever attempt to abuse me in any way.

After completing high school I went for a vocational evaluation with a psychologist. I loved what she was doing, and for the first time I became aware of the field of psychology and was very intrigued. I told the psychologist that I loved science, and she responded with encouragement, telling me that I certainly had the skills to embark on a scientific career. Walking home that day I started to think about becoming a professor in math or chemistry. I enrolled myself in a university program to become a high school math and physics teacher and continued with it for a year. Still, I couldn't stop thinking about how interesting it would be to have a job like that of the psychologist with whom I had met. That could be me someday if I chose that path!

So after a year of majoring in science, I changed my career objective and began to study psychology. At that point I was mature enough to consider what I really wanted to do in life, rather than only thinking in terms of my present skills. I was wising up and beginning to focus on my mission in life—to help people with their problems and guide them at different stages in their lives, as that psychologist had done with me. A dream and a goal were born.

Although my mother was delighted that I was pursuing a higher education, she was 100 percent against my going into a career as a psychologist. Having never had any contact with a psychologist or a psychiatrist at that time in her life, she felt that psychologists ran the risk of taking on the problems of others, and she was concerned that sooner or later I would become deeply troubled myself. As for my father, he wondered why I needed a career at this point, since I had a boyfriend who was in medical school. "Why do you need to work for a living if you're going to marry a doctor?" he asked me. On the other hand, he was very proud of me for having such lofty goals. He just didn't really trust that I would complete a program of study and have a career. But I believed in myself. I got a job and paid for my own university education.

Actually, my enthusiasm and my persistence in striving for a rewarding career had to do with the very qualities my parents had instilled in me. My father had a passion for everything in life, and he passed that wonderful trait on to me. He taught all of us kids that there were no barriers, that we could do whatever we wanted to do and be our own bosses. He was also streetwise. He gave me the sense that if I didn't know something, I could learn it, rather than depend on other people. He showed me how to take risks and to never tell myself "no." And he taught me another very important thing, for which I am immensely grateful: how to be proud of my own achievements, even when they were minor. To praise myself.

And my mother? She was always a hard worker; nothing could prevent her from doing what needed to be done to keep our family together. She worked from early in the morning until late at night—at home and helping my dad with his business. And as much as she talked about marriage and family being important things for a woman, she repeatedly told me when I was a child and a teenager that going to school is the most exciting time in your life. Being in school as a young girl was certainly the happiest, most fulfilling time in her own life, and she had yearned to pursue her education further. But her ambition had been thwarted, so despite her reservations about my career, she was glad for me that I had continued what she had only begun. She always told me "You can lose many things in life—money, people that you love, jobs—but you can never lose your education. What you learn in life belongs to you." The way my mother talked to me about her own experiences, I got the message that getting an education meant "getting the power." And that message continues to inspire me.

Although they initially had doubts about where I was headed and hadn't envisioned for me the kind of career I ended up pursuing, my parents were incredibly proud of me as I strove to reach my goals. My father never had expected such achievements from me. He hadn't really encouraged or motivated me to go to college, because it wasn't a realistic concept for him. Women in professions were the rare exception at that time in Argentina, and he never thought that I could be that exceptional. For my father several decades ago, "a woman was supposed to be a woman" and remain in the home. But when I got my doctorate and became a psychologist, he would tell everyone, "Oh, meet my daughter; she is a doctor." He was also very proud of my brother Bruno, who has a Ph.D. as well (in business administration), but having a daughter who was a doctor—wow! He bragged about me because to him my accomplishment as a woman was so unusual and, therefore so wonderful! As my achievements expanded—having a private practice in Buenos Aires and becoming director of psychology at the Instituto Uriburu there; later opening my private practice in Los Angeles, Riverside, and Orange Counties, heading a nonprofit organization and working within the Latino community here; hosting my radio and television talk shows, *Aquí Entre Nos;* writing my weekly column for *La Opinión;* writing my first book; giving numerous workshops and conference presentations—his and my mom's pride in me expanded as well.

Getting a higher education is a concept that is—or was—unfamiliar to some Latino parents, so some of them cannot envision it either for themselves or for their children. And because they can't foresee the possibility of their daughters and sons attaining such high academic goals, they don't motivate their children to strive for them. If this is the case in your family, I want to tell you one very important thing: It doesn't matter. You don't need to be told "Go to college, head up your own company, or develop your creativity." You don't need to be told what your goals should be. Certainly it can be empowering when your family encourages you to pursue your goals. But if they don't, you can motivate yourself. You can find role models, you can point yourself in the direction you choose, and you can work toward a life you design for yourself.

As you think about your dreams and the goals you want to attain to make them a reality, they may seem very different from the expectations put forth by society or your family. I think you'll discover as you read further, however, that some of your greatest strengths come from those who raised you and were closest to you. Our objective is to put those strengths to work in such a way that you can realize your full and magnificent Latina Power!

The 7 Strengths

Although we Latinas already possess the traits that can help us attain more success in life, we are not always aware of our natural gifts and how to use them. Before I introduce you to the 7 Latina Power Strengths I'd like to place them in context by reviewing Carl Jung's notion of archetypes and the collective unconscious.

Carl Jung, an early disciple of Sigmund Freud, expanded the notion of the unconscious to include the "collective unconscious," which contains those acts and mental patterns shared either by members of a culture or universally by all human beings. He talked about how these mental patterns are arranged as archetypes, images and symbols that are seen in dreams or fantasies and that appear as themes in mythology, religion, and fairy tales. Archetypes are deep and abiding presences in the human psyche that remain powerful throughout our lives. They may even be coded into the makeup of the human brain.

While all human beings share key archetypal patterns, archetypes can vary according to culture. We can identify the archetypes in our own culture by observing the strengths we Latinas have in common: how we act; how we interpret our reality; how we shape our lives and the lives of our families. Although there are more than seven such archetypes or strengths, I selected seven because in my experience and in interviewing successful Latinas, I found these to be the essential ones we possess and which can help us to develop our fullest potential.

These core strengths define our ability to be who we are, our style of interacting with our family and other people, our relationships with our environment and society, and the manifestations of our spirituality. By exploring them, we can become more aware of our essential identities and what our greatest potentials might be. It's fascinating to consider that these strengths, or archetypes, have been in our culture for centuries. But while our personal and cultural histories have influenced our psychological makeups in this way, we now can have a more direct influence on how these strengths play out in our lives.

As you read about the 7 Latina Power Strengths, you will recognize them immediately. They will be as familiar to you as members of your family, because they are aspects of you. Some of these traits may already be well developed within you, due to the influence of your family or your spiritual or social environment. But each of them needs some reinforcement to be working actively to our advantage, to the point where we feel authentically fulfilled and happy with who we are. We have a choice. We can stick complacently with the status quo and neglect to develop these precious traits to the fullest. Or we can work consciously toward making these strengths dominant in our lives so that we become the *mujeres* we were meant to be.

We women like to talk about potential. We tend to see the potential in everybody else, especially in the men in our lives. But it's often hard for us to see our own. Latinas tend to be so humble that we don't recognize our most promising or impressive qualities until someone else points them out to us. We seem to believe that if we acknowledge our strengths we will be perceived as *pretenciosas*. But this acknowledgment of who we are and what we can become can be the first step in expanding and enriching our lives. As you'll discover throughout the book, these strengths are aspects of our true selves, and they can lead us to our greatest potential if we invest our energy into developing them.

This journey of self-discovery may be intimidating because it will require you to reconsider your own identity. However, there is no reason to fear that you will stop being yourself; rather, you will expand the truth of who you are by considering new possibilities and opening yourself to unexplored ideas and experiences. In fact, the journey is never completed. In a truly involved life, we continue to discover aspects of ourselves that we can help to flower and flourish—and this process becomes the challenging adventure that life is intended to be.

So let's now examine these powerful strengths that we've all inherited from our culture and families—and see how they can help us to blossom and succeed.

1: *Espíritu Creativo* (Creative Spirit)

Latinas always have had to use their creativity in order to survive. Whether it was finding a way to stretch our income, improving our economic circumstances by moving to another country or another town, struggling against political persecution, securing better opportunities for our children, or using our creativity to deal with an unsupportive or abusive spouse or family member, Latinas have proven over and over again that a creative spirit can overcome just about any problem or barrier.

Creativity also is related to intuition, which seems to be intrinsic to all women. Our intuition helps us tap into our *espíritu creativo*, and we use it to choose creatively what is best for us. It has been said that every woman has an extra, or "sixth," sense—that of intuition. And it's true. It's not that men don't have it; it's just that women, because we have been trained to be more in touch with our emotions and our inner selves, are more aware of our intuitive powers. It is my belief that Latinas have an especially strong intuitive sense because we enjoy a particularly close connection to nature, the ultimate creative force.

In addition to our intuitive strengths and our use of creativity to survive life's challenges, most Latinas—approximately 80 percent—

have the added benefit of being a creative blend of European and Native American cultures, which means that they tend to have a broad perspective on life. They not only have the ability to understand more than one cultural reality, but similar to children of intermarriages, they embody two traditions and therefore are likely to draw upon their creative spirits in order to integrate both. *Mestizos* are a unique race, and I believe that their inheritance of two distinct cultures feeds their inclination toward creativity.

Creativity isn't just about being an artist or a writer. Being creative leads us to new ideas and to transforming them into action. We can use our *espíritu creativo* to envision our personal goals and come up with ingenious ways to turn dreams into reality. Imagine how you might shape your own future by becoming more intuitive and more creative in thinking about your options. As you become more aware of your strengths and more acquainted with your inner self, your creative spirit will help guide you to the pursuits that fit with who you are.

When you recall the goals you set as a young person, think about whether they reflected your own dreams or the messages you got from your parents or society. To what extent was your *espíritu creativo* involved? There is no limit to how far your creative vision can take you—if you let it.

2: The *Aguantadora*'s Passionate Determination

This trait is derived from the personal experiences of generations of Latinos who have had to endure hardship. *Tenacidad de aguantar las dificultades de la vida,* or tenacity in enduring life's difficulties, is even referred to in the Aztec codices, a systematic description of Aztec ideals and values written from the perspective of the Aztec nobility, which described the most important virtues parents ought to teach their daughters. An *aguantadora*'s attitude is crucial for enduring life's obstacles and remaining passionately focused on your aspirations.

A common belief is that if you're determined enough, and you work hard enough, you can reach whatever goals you envision. We Latinas have an edge when it comes to determination and working hard, because we're brought up to be *aguantadoras*—to be resilient in the face of obstacles and to persevere no matter what. Latino culture continues to teach us to endure and persist, and we do so automatically, without bitterness. In fact, most of us are passionate in our determination to work hard and get ahead.

But whereas in the past many Latinas interpreted *"Aguántate, mujer"* or "Endure, woman" to mean we should simply endure hardships and "take it," now we are using our tenacity to reach our own personal goals. Throughout their lives, our *abuelas* and mothers have embodied the *aguantadora's* perseverance. As you come to acknowledge your history and strengths, you'll feel more resilient and more able to confront whatever disappointments or hardships you may encounter on your path. And you'll be inspired to use your *aguantadora's* drive to go after the new goals you've set for yourself.

3: The *Comadre*'s Networking Ability

Sometimes I think Latinas were the ones to invent networking. Whenever our families or communities need help, we reach out to each other, put our *cabezas* together and figure out the most effective way to solve our problems. We employ our networking skills each time we make arrangements to take care of each other's children or provide help to the sick and elderly in our families and neighborhoods. As Latinas we've learned how to be resourceful by making use of our close female contacts—our closely connected group of *amigas* and neighbors. And we get the job done!

But are we as savvy when it comes to using our *comadre* network to further our personal goals? If it's true that networking is one of the most essential skills on the path to success, then there's no excuse for any Latina to be left behind, because counseling and helping, conferring and organizing with our *comadres* comes naturally for us. Later in the book we'll go into more detail about how you can utilize your *comadre* networking skills in order to develop the life you aspire to. You'll discover how relatives, friends, and community contacts can become a valuable *comadre* network of support. We'll be talking about how you can form "*comadre* circles" that empower members to pursue their life goals, accomplish political objectives, heal from traumatic life events, and more.

Also, whether you're interested in starting up a business, finding a mentor who can guide you in making beneficial career moves, or identifying people who can advise you regarding educational options, it's all about being connected, no? And we Latinas have been connecting all our lives because our culture encourages women to foster a nurturing bond and help each other out. Our *abuelitas* and moms always have benefited from the strength and spiritual dimensions of their female friendships, and now we can use this meaningful way of relating to our *comadres* to help each other go after our life goals.

4: The *Diplomática's* Discretion

Diplomacy is a trait we've inherited because women have had to be the diplomats within large extended families. With so many divergent opinions being expressed in nearly every Latino family, isn't it usually we women who find a way to create a common ground and bring people together? Learning from our mothers, *tías*, and grandmothers how to smooth things over among family members is part of every Latina's upbringing. In our culture women are expected to bridge the gap between warring family factions so that *la familia* is preserved.

Diplomacia plays an equally important role in every endeavor where human beings have to get along and deal with each other, whether it's you and your college professor, the other members of your law firm or community organization, your fellow congresswomen and -men, or the customers who come into your restaurant. Knowing how to communicate diplomatically and effectively with coworkers, clients, students, or bosses—despite conflicting perspectives—can mean the difference between losing the trust of those with whom you work and forging strong relationships that ensure your success. We've learned to be *diplomáticas* in our families; now we can use our talent for tact and discretion to benefit our lives outside the home.

5: The *Atrevida*'s Courage

Sticking to the safest, most well-worn path is not the way Latinas go through life. Perhaps it is because we have had to be courageous and take risks in order to survive, so we're prepared to face the unexpected. From generation to generation our people often have had to uproot themselves, to seek work in foreign cities, towns, or even countries, and learn to adapt to new customs. Our parents and grandparents had the courage to carve out new lives for themselves, often against great odds.

As women we know that in order to survive sometimes we must be an *atrevida*. We never would let our children suffer, and we therefore do whatever is necessary for them to have a better life than we may have had. We don't think twice about searching for a way to make that happen, even if it involves personal risk. We're able to tap into the *atrevida* side of ourselves because, as Latinas, we have a brave heritage and we carry that within us.

As well, we have the experience of having had to fight certain personal battles courageously. Very often we've had to rebel against what our family or our culture has told us is "appropriate" for women in order to follow our own mission in life. Having the guts and the energy to say "I'm going to become an *atrevida* and take an alternate route" makes us strong. And we can use this empowering trait to take productive risks in our careers. Having the courage to take those chances that could bring us closer to our dreams can mean the difference between stagnating and thriving.

Being an *atrevida* is not only about taking risks, though; it's also about having a goal and taking consistent, bold steps toward it. If you take only safe steps, chances are you'll never develop new skills or fulfill your potential. Rather, you'll be like a child with an overprotective mother, listening only to your cautious inner voice and perpetuating the myth that women are the *sexo débil*.

Later you'll get a chance to discover how much of an *atrevida* you have been and are willing to become in order to move forward with your life's dreams and goals. We'll also talk about the important differences between a wise risk and an unwise one, so that you understand when to take chances in your career and when to hold back and wait for better opportunities.

6: The *Malabarista*'s Balance

Our ability to balance responsibilities comes naturally to us because as Latinas we must juggle a variety of duties to our immediate families, our extended families, and our communities. Learning how to apportion our time between family and career is especially important for Latinas, for whom family is always a priority.

As Latinas we are taught to balance our commitments to our parents, spouse, children, extended families, communities, and spiritual life. Although it often seems overwhelming, we somehow manage to accomplish all the things that are expected of us. Many Latinas are now incorporating another element into this balancing act: dedication to oneself, giving oneself the time and space to develop personal goals, which often include a higher education and a career.

We each can learn to enhance our sense of balance so that we have the energy and the time to devote to both our family and our work outside the home. This balancing of *trabajo y familia* is extremely important, because otherwise we unconsciously may sabotage our success as a way to assuage our guilt for being working mothers and wives. It is equally important that we strive for and maintain a sense of inner balance, which can only be achieved when we give enough time to ourselves and to those things that make us feel whole.

7: *La Reina*'s Confidence and Strength

A belief in ourselves as *reinas* stems from our culture's reverence for and reliance on women. It always has been our designated role to be competent and strong, to make family decisions, and to transmit our culture to our children. We also can use our queenly confidence, wisdom, and sense of responsibility in a spiritual manner to enhance all other aspects of our lives, including our professional or business capabilities.

The Latino culture always has taught its girls that a woman's highest achievement is to become *reina del hogar.* Although this sounded great in the past, many Latinas began to wonder "Is that all there is?" We now realize that there is much more to life than home, and that it is now every Latina's option to extend her *reinado* to the world outside her family. We have options all around us and can create opportunities where none seemed to exist before.

Although Latinas are beginning to assume positions of power throughout the world, Latino culture continues to be ambivalent about the essential value of women. On the one hand, women have had limited power outside the home. On the other, every Latino man honors his mother, sometimes to the point of viewing her as the embodiment of the Virgin Mary or the Virgen de Guadalupe. A woman's sons and daughters come to her for advice, wisdom, and warmth. The term *reina del hogar* signifies the strongest female position of power within the household, and the respect and sense of prominence that go along with that role give women an inner strength and confidence.

A Latina's inner sense of self-worth, derived from the high value our culture places on her role within the home, can be shifted over to developing our power as *reinas* in every aspect of our lives. As you continue to read this book, you'll learn how to transfer your queenly position from your home to your chosen field of endeavor outside the home. Ultimately, becoming *la reina* you were meant to be is about feeling "worth it" in the broadest sense of the word. It's about feeling that you're worthy of owning and fulfilling your own dreams.

A Few Precautions as You Begin This Powerful Journey

Although we've been discussing the positive aspects of each Latina Power strength, we also should be aware that over- or underemphasizing any one of these qualities can have a negative impact. We can refer to this harmful outcome as the "shadow side" of each strength. Too much *atrevida* risk-taking, for example, may result in unwise decisions or unnecessary losses; too little can hold you back from pursuing your dreams. Being overly diplomatic may cause you to withhold a truth that needs to be expressed, while too little diplomacy can cause you to alienate those with whom you're dealing. Balance will be the key in developing your Latina Power strengths so that they serve you in the best possible way. Throughout the book I will point out the shadow sides of each strength, what to watch out for, and steps you can take to insure that you embody the seven archetypes in a balanced way.

You should also know that you may encounter some negative reactions as you begin your journey toward becoming a more powerful woman. In this process of developing yourself, you may find that other people are disapproving. This is usually because changes can produce fear of the unknown. We are heading into a new role for ourselves, and that can create considerable anxiety in others, which can in turn lead to their resistance to our plans. In their effort to try to protect us — because women are supposed to be protected in the Latino culture — our families or our spouses may try to hold us back from what they think could harm us. This is a justifiable motive, but the reality is that we don't need to be protected from choosing what we want in life. Being protected, in this case, means being restricted.

If this scenario rings true for you, you will need to decide if you want to give in to the fears that others may have or continue to pursue your own vision. In contrast to what we've always been told—that doing things for others is more important than doing them for ourselves—developing our powerful strengths is a process we unapologetically engage in for our own betterment. No one needs to agree with you; nobody needs to support you; nobody needs to endorse what you're doing. This is a journey that requires only a one-person send-off committee: you.

What We Mean by "Power"

The meaning of the word "power" also needs clarifying so that we're thinking about it in a way that is most beneficial to our personal growth as well as to the communities, cities, and nations of which we are part. By becoming powerful we are not aiming to have power over anyone else or to displace other groups of people. Sociologists define power as the ability to influence others, and this can take many forms: a politician's power, a writer's power, a businesswoman's power, a scientist's power, an artist's power, a mother's power. Latina Power is about our desire and ability to fulfill our human potential, to influence and empower other Latinas with the examples our lives provide, and to thereby enhance the world community to which we belong.

As women we are keenly aware of the fact that our gender has not always wielded power outside the home. And as Latinas in particular we have struggled with the constraint our culture has placed on us by advocating that we be content with our role as *reina del hogar*, just as many of our aunts and mothers and grandmothers seemed to be. We were told that it was our duty to be mothers and housewives exclusively, to transmit our values and culture to our children, and that these important roles negated the need to be involved in the world. But the women's movement instigated sweeping changes that would have seemed impossible to our *abuelitas*. These fundamental institutional and cultural shifts have resulted in today's women being able to pursue careers in whatever fields we choose. The last thirty years have seen gender barriers broken down, new opportunities made available to us, and women from all classes and ethnic backgrounds working hard to take advantage of those opportunities. In 1960, in the United States, only 60 percent of women had graduated from high school; in 1995, 88 percent of women had. Less than 35 percent of women were in the United States workforce in 1960 and now, according to the 2000 U.S. Census Bureau statistics, 61 percent of non-Hispanic white women and 57 percent of Hispanic women are. Ten years ago, there were no Latinas in the U.S. Congress; today there are seven. And more than one-third of Latino-owned businesses in the United States are owned by Latinas.

By participating in the decision-making functions of government, the corporate world, education, etc., Latinas are beginning to share the power in this and other countries, and the institutions that shape our society are thus beginning to incorporate a female and a Latina per-spective.

And yet, women in the United States, arguably among the most liberated in the world, still earn only 73 percent of what a man earns for the same job. And the percentage is even lower for Latinas: 52 per-cent. Only 25 percent of U.S. lawyers, 23 percent of architects, 22 per-cent of physicians, 10 percent of engineers, and 2 percent of the CEOs of the largest corporations in the United States are women. According to recent statistics from the U.S. Department of Labor, Latinas are most heavily concentrated in clerical and service occupations, and the income of Latinas is less than that of any other group. Thirteen percent of all women are living in poverty, with African-American and His-panic women having the highest poverty rates among adults. Most recently, women have been affected adversely by the economic re-structuring and job displacement of the early twenty-first century. In addition, only 10 percent of Latinas in the United States have four years or more of higher education, compared with 24 percent of non-Hispanic white women.

So we have our work cut out for us. Becoming a powerful Latina and helping to empower others will require intense effort. We rise to the challenge knowing that the power we seek will enrich not only our own lives but the lives of all those who share the dream of becoming who they were meant to be.

Meeting Your *Comadres*

Using the 7 strengths to create a fulfilling and meaningful life for yourself, your family, and your community is what Latina Power is all about. It's also about creating a community of *comadres*, and in the course of this book you'll be meeting some fascinating women who will come to feel like your sisters or closest friends. They've experienced some of the same challenges you've faced, from being raised in poverty or having to flee a repressive country and adjust to a new one, to being discriminated against or disregarded by those who didn't believe a woman or a Latina could achieve what they set out to accomplish. And yet each of these women has triumphed in her own powerful way. You'll see yourself in their struggles and be inspired by their stories.

The Latinas you'll meet are from such diverse fields as molecular biology, toy design, entertainment, social activism, journalism, sports, government, and *curanderismo*. Their national and ethnic origins range from Mexico, Cuba, and Puerto Rico to Central and South America. What they have in common with each other and with you are their family values, their history, their cultural perspective as Latinas (although of course these vary somewhat according to one's national origin) and their embodiment of the empowering strengths that comprise Latina Power. I am certain you will feel a bond with these women, as I certainly did when I interviewed them. Each of them expressed the desire to share their stories with you as a way of widening the *comadre* circle to which we all belong.

The 7 Latina Power Strengths Self-Evaluation Test

At this point, I'd like to invite you to take the "7 Latina Power Strengths Self-Evaluation Test," which will help you evaluate the presence of the seven strengths in your own approach to life. Evaluating your responses, you'll be able to see which empowering traits are working for you already and which may require further development. It is important that we become more aware of the strengths we have inherited from our culture so that we can use them more effectively to enhance our careers and our personal lives.

By integrating what we've learned as Latinas in our families and communities — by using our *espíritu creativo,* our *aguantadora's* fortitude, our networks of *comadres,* our talent for diplomacy, our ability to be courageous *atrevidas* and well-balanced *malabaristas,* and our belief in ourselves as *reinas* — we can more effectively shape what we want to become.

Discover which Latina Power strengths are most dominant in your life by indicating how frequently the following statements reflect your attitude. Score each statement using the following zero-to-four criteria: Never: 0; Seldom: 1; Sometimes: 2; Frequently: 3; Always: 4.

After completing the test, total up the points in each strength column and take the time to examine the traits that are currently most active in your life. Less than 12 points indicates that you need to develop that strength. Twelve or more points suggests that that particular strength is active in your life but could be enhanced; 16 or more means that it is very active; and 20 or more means . . . you've got it! You've got the power!

As you continue to read *Latina Power,* you'll find out how to implement all seven strengths, each of which can empower you to have more success and fulfillment in your life. You will discover that these qualities are within you already and that all you need to do is acknowledge their presence and activate their power.

1. ____ I enjoy the challenge and the freedom of doing things my way.
2. ____ I believe that success has no gender.
3. ____ My parents taught me how to be responsible, and I can use this sense of responsibility in other endeavors in life, such as work or a career.
4. ____ I understand that my success may require my partner to make adjustments he is not ready to make. I am determined to work on this challenge without holding myself back or compromising my integrity.
5. ____ I believe that I have the power to design my own future, even against unfavorable odds.
6. ____ When something doesn't go my way, I persist, because I know that in the long run I will reach my destination.
7. ____ I have an easy time trusting other women (who deserve my trust).
8. ____ When I get angry, I am aware that it is my reaction to something that I consider unfair. Instead of blaming the other person for making me angry, I know how to speak up calmly and say what I consider to be wrong.
9. ____ I know how much I am willing to invest for what I want to accomplish in life—and that investment doesn't intimidate me.
10. ____ I see myself as a strong, confident person who can do anything she sets her mind to.
11. ____ When a door closes on me, I call on myself to explore new ways to reach my goals.
12. ____ When I want something, I work hard enough to get it, even when I see that it might be difficult.
13. ____ I know how to choose the right time, place, and tone in which to express my opinions.
14. ____ I understand that balancing home, relationship, and career may not be easy, but I'm committed to finding workable solutions.
15. ____ I believe that I can rely on myself first and foremost.
16. ____ I pursue the ideas that I come up with, even when others think they are unworthy.
17. ____ When I feel that I am failing, I think about instances when I felt the same way and was able to succeed.

18. ____ When I need help, I ask for it.

19. ____ When someone looks down on me for being a Latina, I know how to politely yet firmly stand up for myself.

20. ____ Whenever I encounter a valuable opportunity, I am determined to take the risk.

21. ____ I've learned that I'm multifaceted and can balance different aspects of my life, such as family, relationship, and work, without having to choose one over the other.

22. ____ I am able to create my own balance in life, even though it might be different from others'.

23. ____ I believe that I am able to earn a living by myself and that I can ensure my own and my family's welfare.

24. ____ I have a vision of what I want for my life, but I'm not afraid of changing that vision to adapt to new circumstances and ideas.

25. ____ Whenever my internal voice tells me "You can't do that" I take it as a challenge and find a way to continue going ahead with my plans.

26. ____ I feel motivated and stimulated by other successful Latinas.

27. ____ I know that it is as wise to remain silent as to speak up, depending on the situation.

28. ____ I am a good listener, because I know that's how I can learn more about people.

29. ____ Even when other people tell me I might fail, I stay focused and try that much harder to succeed.

30. ____ I am aware that I have to take good care of myself before I can take care of others.

31. ____ I know that I have a responsibility to my family, but I also have a responsibility to myself and to my community.

32. ____ I own my dreams, and I am responsible for making them materialize.

33. ____ My intuition often provides me with the insight to make wise decisions.

34. ____ I feel passionate when I'm working hard toward a desired goal.

35. ____ I am part of a supportive network of people whom I can call on for advice and assistance.

36. ____ I know how to find common ground with those whose opinions differ from mine.

37. ____ I have one special *amiga* or *comadre* in whom I can confide and who I know will be there for me as I am there for her.

38. ____ I realize that sometimes I have to curtail my plans and wait for better opportunities so that I won't take any unwise risks.

39. ____ I believe I am a valuable person and that I can be rewarded for my abilities accordingly.

40. ____ I believe that a fulfilling life consists of a healthy relationship with my partner, quality time with my family, and engaging in pursuits that I find rewarding.

41. ____ I give myself permission to succeed in everything I envision.

42. ____ When something goes wrong, I give myself a second chance.

43. ____ I am aware of how my community can help me achieve success.

44. ____ I've learned that *chismes* can destroy people's trust in me—and that forgoing gossip can be the key to receiving someone's trust.

45. ____ I usually do something because I want to do it, not because it's expected of me.

46. ____ When I am presented with a dilemma, I have the ability to see things from a broad perspective.

47. ____ I believe that Latinas can work together for the benefit of our families and communities.

48. ____ When I believe in something, I go for it—even when I have been told that it's not appropriate for women or for Latinas.

49. ____ When I know I'm working too hard, I speak up and delegate my responsibilities.

[ANSWERS ON THE FOLLOWING PAGE]

Espíritu Creativo

#1 _____

#5 _____

#11 _____

#16 _____

#24 _____

#33 _____

#41 _____

total _____

Aguantadora's Passionate
Determination

#6 _____

#12 _____

#17 _____

#25 _____

#34 _____

#42 _____

#49 _____

total _____

Comadre's Networking Ability

#7 _____

#18 _____

#26 _____

#35 _____

#37 _____

#43 _____

#47 _____

total _____

Diplomática's Discretion

#8 _____

#13 _____

#19 _____

#27 _____

#28 _____

#36 _____

#44 _____

total _____

Atrevida's Courage

#2 _____

#9 _____

#20 _____

#29 _____

#38 _____

#45 _____

#48 _____

total _____

Malabarista's Balance

#4 _____

#14 _____

#21 _____

#22 _____

#30 _____

#40 _____

#46 _____

total _____

La Reina's Confidence and Strength

#3 _____

#10 _____

#15 _____

#23 _____

#31 _____

#32 _____

#39 _____

Total _____

2

Espíritu Creativo

Our intuition is part of our inner power, which enables us to believe
in our ability to make miracles.

I always wanted to have my own business, and I told my father
this, but he discouraged me, insisting that business is not for a
woman. But I had a voice inside me since I was seven years old—and
we all have this wise, creative voice inside—saying, "Listen to yourself. Life is like a movie and you are the director. Take control!"

—Leticia Herrera, chair, Extra Clean Inc.,
and regional chair for the United States
Hispanic Chamber of Commerce

You don't have to be an artist or a musician to "make miracles" or lead
a creative life. We are all born with a powerful creative impulse. For a
variety of reasons that we're going to explore, Latinas in particular are
called upon to use this inherent *espíritu creativo*. In this chapter we're
going to discover how to use our natural sense of creativity in order to
envision the career and the future we want for ourselves. Along the
way we'll meet Latinas who are passionately engaged in various occupational pursuits—political organizing, toy design, cosmetics sales,
cartooning, architectural restoration, and the healing arts. The common denominator in their stories is that their *espíritu creativo* was instrumental in guiding them toward their goals.

Your Latino heritage contains the roots for being a *creativa*, because your ancestors frequently had to use their ingenuity to deal with
hardships. Faced with poverty, racism, and other barriers to opportunity your parents and grandparents have always found creative ways
to break down society's roadblocks. It turns out that this ability to use

your *espíritu creativo* to solve problems is one of the hallmarks of being a creative person, according to those who study creativity. In his book *Creativity: Flow and the Psychology of Discovery and Invention,* Professor Mihaly Csikszentmihalyi of the University of Chicago tells us that what makes creative individuals remarkable is their ability to adapt to almost any situation and to make do with whatever is at hand to reach their goals. Rather than calling upon only one way of thinking or one way of acting when faced with a particular challenge, creative people, says Professor Csikszentmihalyi, have a more "complex personality" which enables them to draw from a wider repertoire of ideas and actions. Whereas most people tend to gravitate to one type of behavior or another, creative people have the ability to express the full range of traits that potentially are present in every human being.

Because Latinos have had to employ creative resources to deal with the many challenges they've faced, and to use more than one method for getting around the barriers placed in their path, this "complex," creative personality describes us quite accurately. We Latinas consistently use our *espíritu creativo* to solve problems within our families and to make life better in our communities. In this chapter we're going to expand on that traditional use of creativity. We're going to discover how to draw from our inner creative spirit in order to design our own future. Perhaps you've never really believed you could become the director of your own life, calling the shots so that your life truly reflects who you are and what you want to accomplish. But you have the power to do just that. Regardless of your personal circumstances, when you envision what it is you want, when you can place yourself into that vision, and when you take realistic steps to get there, your life expands. Even though you may not arrive at precisely the place you initially had in mind, your vision and your efforts will enable you to thrive. And this process all begins with your *espíritu creativo.* By employing our intuition and ingenuity—and balancing them with sound information about our options—we can creatively set goals that fit who we are and what we want to do with our lives.

A Creative Spirit and a Latina's Connection to Nature
Curandera Elena Avila

An element that is integral to a Latina's *espíritu creativo* is her deep sense of connectedness to nature. The original and ultimate source of creativity, nature inspires us and allows us to see the potential of something springing miraculously from what appears to be nothing, but is in fact the energy from which we all derive. Indigenous people throughout the world always have held to the concept of an interconnectedness and interdependence between everything in nature, including human beings. Because most Latinos trace their roots to indigenous cultures, they tend to enjoy this close relationship to nature. And it allows them access to their creative spirit, since they feel themselves to be part of the very essence of creativity.

One woman who beautifully embodies this creative connection is Elena Avila, who explained to me this essential relationship that every Latina has to nature. A registered nurse with a master's degree in psychiatric nursing, she runs a full-time practice as a professional *curandera*. Her book, *Woman Who Glows in the Dark*, offers readers a look into the world of *curanderismo* and how it can contribute to one's physical and emotional wellness. In our conversation Elena described Latino traditions as "earthy," which is why they tend to foster such an inspiring relationship to nature and feed one's creative impulses. "Human beings are very creative—it's our natural state," she told me. "And I think our Latino traditions keep us in touch with nature. I don't know whether it comes from our Spanish ancestors or indigenous ancestors, but I think Latinas are taught that we are not just a part of nature, we *are* nature."

In her work as a *curandera*, Elena created an altar for her treatment room. The altar is important, she says, because it acts as a focus for the sacred. On the screen behind her altar is a three-paneled painting, each panel depicting one aspect of female energy. On one of the panels is Coyolxauhqui, an Aztec goddess who represents the moon. According to legend, she went into battle with her brothers, the stars, against Huitzilopochtli, the sun, in order to restore balance to the universe. Coyolxauhqui thus signifies the balance between moon and sun, and earth and sky, and the divine energy that resides in all human beings. For Elena, this goddess represents the idea that all women have more than one aspect to their nature, one of which is creativity.

In *Woman Who Glows in the Dark* Elena talks about the significance of Coyolxauhqui, who when pregnant is a symbol of creativity.

> All women are living embodiments of the creative force, and every woman understands the transformation of maternity, whether we are giving birth to flesh-and-blood children or to the children of our hearts—art, music, dance, painting, books. As we struggle in our personal battles, at times we all feel her *descoyuntada*—her dislocation and fatigue. But she also teaches us that when we go into battle, when we pass through the delivery of whatever we need to give birth to, we emerge transformed.

Using elements of nature—herbs, plants, a natural diet, her own healing energy in the form of massage, body work, psychological and spiritual insight—Elena helps clients bring about their own physical or emotional transformations. Her reliance on her intimate relationship to nature was made poignantly clear in a life-changing creative experience she told me about. It involved trying to work through an unhappy personal history with her mother. She was in the desert in El Paso. It was evening, when the sunsets are brilliant and the smell of the creosote bush is intense. Elena covered herself with *la arena,* as she has done since she was a child. And then she was suddenly struck with an important spiritual insight: "I had an awareness that, even though I didn't have a loving mother, the Earth is also my mother. For the first time in my life, I wrote a poem, and part of the poem is 'Mamá, mamá, I'm back'—and I was talking to the Earth."

So the first time this talented *curandera* was inspired to write a poem, she was rolling in the dirt, in the sand, speaking directly to *la madre tierra*. The voice that arose in Elena, the one that intuitively knew the essential truth about who she is, that creative voice, is in each of us. When we cultivate and nurture our relationship to nature, we can hear it too.

Our experiences in nature need not be as dramatic as rolling in the desert sand, and they can take place regardless of the environment we live in. Walking on the beach and letting the sea give you its rhythmic wisdom, watching the clouds move across the sky from your porch or apartment window, showing a child where birds have built their nest—each of these ordinary ways to be attentive to nature can help foster an extraordinary creative relationship. Nature is dazzling us constantly with its myriad textures, scents, shapes, colors, and changes. It epitomizes creativity—and our close connection to the forces of nature can inspire us to paint deserts and move mountains in our own life.

Julz Chávez's "Get Real Girl" Dolls
Taking a Creative Leap

While it's important to appreciate the creative spirit we inherit from our Latino cultures, many of us have also felt restricted by the limited choices Latinas sometimes seem to be offered. Teacher, nurse, secretary—these have traditionally been the acceptable careers for a Latina. Women who have dared to break out of these traditional roles are sometimes looked upon as having abandoned their roots. And yet the more Latinas who creatively design their own path and make their own way in the world, the easier it becomes for others to do so as well.

Julz Chávez, who has developed a line of liberated dolls for girls, is a vibrant example of someone who is using her *espíritu creativo* to leap beyond gender stereotypes and provide new inspiration to the younger generation. Her "Get Real" multiethnic, athletic dolls— who surf, ski, snowboard, skateboard, play basketball and soccer—

embody the spirit of being your own role model by actively engaging in the challenge and adventure of sports. These empowering action figures are not only competing in the Barbie marketplace to rave reviews, but they promote Julz's deeply held belief in sports as a confidence builder for young girls.

One of eleven children, Julz is the daughter of a Mexican-American migrant farmworker and the second cousin to labor organizer and human rights activist César Chávez. During our conversation she talked about the unique gifts she received from her father, her childhood curiosity, and the creative links that led to her career as a barrier-breaking doll designer. Her father was the last migrant farmworker of the family, and every summer he would take his children to the fields to show them where they came from. He told them that the reason he worked so hard was so that they could go to college and make a difference. When Julz felt confused in the first grade because her teacher referred to the president of the United States and other famous men as role models, she went home to her father and asked, "Since the president is not a girl, who is *my* role model?" And he told her, "If you want to be president, you can be your own role model. Whatever you want to be, if there's no role model, you can become it yourself." He encouraged Julz and her sisters no less than he did his sons.

Since Julz grew up with five brothers and five sisters, she was often called upon to entertain her siblings. Because she didn't care for the typical fashion-oriented dolls like Barbie ("I never liked her because she didn't look like me or anyone in my family—and she didn't do the kinds of things I wanted to do"), Julz made her own toys to share with her sisters and brothers. Ironically, many years later—after attending California College of Arts and Crafts and holding a number of jobs at other toy companies—she went to work for Mattel, the makers of Barbie. But neither they nor any of the other firms where she worked were interested in developing a new doll that reflected Julz's ideas.

So she decided to create her own company, with the help of her partner, Michael Cookson, and produce a line of empowering dolls herself, a number of which are based on friends who are professional athletes. "I want to encourage girls to participate in sports and to develop their strength and confidence. It's still not common for women to play sports, especially Latinas. Unfortunately, many Latino parents are not supportive of girls going into sports, and I want to change that," she told me.

I mentioned to Julz that perhaps the reason Latino parents don't encourage girls to participate in athletic activities is that they don't consider sports to be feminine. She said, "That's true, but sports gives girls of all ages tremendous confidence." I then came to the conclusion that confidence itself may not be considered by most Latino parents to be a feminine trait. Because, after all, we are supposed to rely on our men, and if we are truly confident within ourselves, we won't need them in that fundamental way anymore. Thankfully, this belief in limiting the potential of girls by neglecting to foster their confidence is not held by all Latino families—certainly not by Julz's father, who was instrumental in nourishing her confidence and her creative spirit, the sparks that lit her Get Real Girl success.

When you consider the life plans you had as a young girl and the ones you have now, do you think they reflect your own dreams, or do they mirror the expectations of your parents, Latino culture, or the society at large? In using your *espíritu creativo* to envision your goals, why not take that creative leap—as Julz did—and allow yourself the complete freedom to see unbounded possibilities!

Leticia Herrera
We Are the Architects of Our Own Lives

I'd like to share Leticia Herrera's story with you now. It beautifully demonstrates that being willing to unleash your *espíritu creativo* can unexpectedly open the door to marvelous new opportunities. One aspect of creativity, which Leticia's story brings out, is the energy and readiness to think on your feet and use all the resources at your disposal to create something that didn't exist before.

"The business that I have now is my true calling," Leticia told me. But she discovered that calling quite by accident. She owed a friend a favor and had to come up with a creative solution in order to repay it. Leticia promised her friend that she would find reliable people to do the janitorial work for this friend's upcoming fundraiser. Having a lot of contacts, Leticia figured it would be easy. But just before the event, the crew she had lined up to do the job called saying they couldn't make it. There was no way Leticia could let her friend down, so she decided to do the work herself.

She had never even done her own housework—and definitely didn't know how to do janitorial work—but in a matter of a day, she opened her business, which is called Extra Clean, Inc. Leticia recalls that "for that event I became the Mexican version of Carol Burnett. I managed to contract people to work with me, we all piled into a van, and we got the job done. It was definitely a burst of creative energy—part of that inner voice that told me I could do this!"

Soon the company evolved into a commercial cleaning business. Eight years ago Leticia was earning a salary of $16,000 a year and today she is the owner of a multimillion-dollar firm. To distinguish her janitorial cleaning business within a crowded field, she eventually chose a highly specialized niche in stone and marble restoration and other specialty cleaning services. "I see architecture as a visible bridge between antiquity and the future," Leticia says, "and I am profoundly moved by the energy that emanates from magnificent public structures. My company is dedicated to maintaining the beauty of these structures, and our message is: 'There's an art to what we do.'"

Although it came about in an unexpected way, Leticia's business is now her true calling—and she discovered it by employing her creative spirit. How might your *espíritu creativo* take you to unexpected places in your life and your career? And how open are you to experimentation?

We all have the gift of life and we each have a mission; it is up to us to develop and use our talents and to find what it is that we are meant to do with our lives. Our sense of experimentation and creativity can help us discover our true calling.

Even if you are presently engaged in work that you don't enjoy that much, there might be a significance to it that will lead you to what you are supposed to be doing. Think about your present situation creatively. Where do your thoughts and ideas lead you? Maybe you will simply come to the realization that you are in the wrong place, which is the first step in getting you off the wrong track and onto the right one. Search inside of yourself for what will bring you joy and a sense of fulfillment. Build your dream—and then become your own architect. And don't forget to consult your intuition.

Exercise: Developing Your Intuition

In order to tap into our creative spirit and envision the path that's right for us, it is important that we develop and learn to trust our intuition. What exactly is intuition? Simply put, it is internal information given to us via our thoughts, emotions, or physical sensations. Since it is a form of perception that is not intellectual, we tend to ignore our intuition, because we live in a society that believes almost exclusively in rational thought. But haven't we all had the experience of sensing some truth about someone or something, then ignoring that internal sense and later discovering that the information our intuition gave us was valid?

As a matter of fact, scientists are beginning to isolate the part of our brain that is responsible for our intuitive abilities. Through his studies of MRI—magnetic resonance imaging—British scientist Christopher Frith has been able to prove that when a person imagines what someone else is thinking or feeling, the frontal area of the cortex responds in a particular way. So this "irrational" internal guide that often can give us very accurate information is now being proven to exist, using very rational means.

How can we use this guide more effectively to help us carve out a path that suits who we are and what we want to do with our lives? We might want to initiate a formal practice for just five minutes a day, a time given over specifically to the nourishment of our intuition. It could include the following steps:

1. Create an altar surrounded by items representing the natural elements air, water, fire, and earth. You might want to have the altar by an open window to feel the breeze and include a glass of water, a candle, and something representing the earth, like a rock, a plant, or a flower. Or choose a place outdoors, where the natural elements are more intrinsic. Use this place to do your intuitive practice each day.

2. Relax your body and free your mind of all the pressures and stimuli of the day.

3. Open up your mind to your internal guide—your intuition—that is an intimate part of yourself. Consider your intuition like a friend you have had for many years, someone you love very much but don't see very often. Welcome that friend.

4. Concentrate on what your body and emotions tell you as you encounter your intuition. For example, if you are considering a decision you have to make, or a particular path you might want to take, visualize your options and then notice your physical and emotional reactions to each of these options. Which path, which decision, makes your body feel most comfortable? Which makes you feel most at peace within yourself? What is your intuition telling you?

Anita Pérez Ferguson's Mother Had a Saying
"Make Something Out of Nothing"

Providing leadership and political skills training to women throughout the world, Anita Pérez Ferguson formerly served in Washington, D.C. as the president of the National Women's Political Caucus and the White House liaison to the U.S. Department of Transportation. When I asked this influential and dynamic woman how she stays focused on the uphill battle of bringing women into the political arena, her first response was to remember the creative wisdom of her mother.

"She always had a saying: 'Make something out of nothing,' meaning, make do with what you have. This has helped me immensely in my work with nonprofit organizations, because resources are nearly always scarce. So I don't get frustrated—I get creative and figure out what I can do to make something from nothing." An interesting example of this creative strategy came about when Anita was working with the National Women's Political Caucus. There was a point at which she was barely able to make payroll and was worried about not being able to continue the group's important work. Knowing there had to be a creative solution somewhere, she gathered together the other leaders of the organization and they did an evaluation of their assets: an office space, a mailing list they could use to plan an event, and a good reputation in Washington, D.C. that they could capitalize on. Their brainstorming resulted in a focus-on-women inaugural ball for President Clinton's second inauguration. They invited all the female appointed and elected federal as well as local officials, the First Lady, and many of the founders of the women's movement. They had only women performers, an all-women band, female singers, even female waiters. "We did invite men too, though—to dance with us!" Anita recalls. With the success of that event Anita and her colleagues made enough money to keep the organization going.

It seems that Anita's mother's creative advice applies as well to the presence of women and Latinas in politics, as Anita explained to me. Ten years ago there were no Latinas in the U.S. Congress. However, from nothing—with the application of focused effort, organizational drive, and *espíritu creativo*—came something. Today there are seven Latinas in the U.S. House of Representatives, and with women like Anita Pérez Ferguson spearheading the movement, more and more likely will be elected in the years to come. What kinds of changes will women and Latinas bring about as they become a stronger presence in our national government? When I asked her that question Anita told me, "It will make a big difference when there are more women in politics, because women have to juggle between work and family in a way that men don't, and their awareness of this has an impact on government at every level. When women work on public policy, they tend to include their personal experiences, as opposed to men who are infrequently involved with family responsibilities. As for Latinas, they will bring a needed perspective to the governmental forum. We have a strong sense of the balance between family and work and a healthy skepticism about government and institutions. We're able to see through ineffective proposals that are supposed to protect the rights of the unprotected but don't. It's important for Latinas to be involved in the process, because we have this sense of what *will* be effective."

A songwriter friend of mine tells me that for her the greatest thrill is to walk into a recording studio and hear the musicians rehearsing her music. Knowing that she has created a song that pleases her and others—that didn't exist before—gives her a sense of joyful fulfillment unmatched by anything else. The exhilarating feeling that comes from making something from nothing, from putting your distinct talents and skills into a project that you believe in, is the fruit of creative experience. And you can enjoy it whether you're a songwriter, a political organizer, a teacher, or a businesswoman.

The Storm That Empowered Martha Montoya's Cartoon Characters

Because creativity requires that you feel free to express your vision—however outrageous it might seem to the outside world—it also requires being fearless. In fact, sometimes your *espíritu creativo* is shaped by frightening or life-threatening incidents, which call on you to reach inside yourself to combat your fear. This was the case in cartoonist Martha Montoya's life.

An immigrant to the United States from Colombia, Martha initially had to put her artistic goals aside. Not knowing anyone and without a place to live, she got a position as a live-in housekeeper in a wealthy household. Her mother had told her, *"Mejor cola de león que cabeza de ratón"* ("better to be a lion's tail than a mouse's head"), so living in a nice environment seemed worth it. It was very hard work, however, and Martha left after three months, turning instead to a job as a librarian. Her vision of using her artistic skills to teach Latino children about their culture eventually became a reality with the success of her cartoon strip, *Los Kitos*, now seen in 305 newspapers nationwide and in seventeen countries throughout the world. When I talked to Martha about the greatest influences in her creative life, she told me the dramatic story of surviving a potentially deadly storm.

When she was fifteen years old and still living in Colombia, Martha went with her father and her aunt by boat to spend the Christmas holiday in the coastal town Santa Marta. (Since the sea was somewhat rough, her mother stayed at home with her little brother.) A short while after they left, the sky turned dark, the ocean became rough, and their boat capsized. Martha and her relatives were forced to spend two nights and three days in the water. There were sharks nearby, and all they could do was hold on to the boat and pray. "The whole experience led me to a lot of questioning," Martha told me. "The main thing was that I realized I had to stay positive. We were finally able to rescue ourselves, constantly pushing the overturned boat until we got to the beach. And from that I learned that you control your own destiny. Because there was no one to help us; we had to do it ourselves."

Martha says that her cartoon strip, *Los Kitos*, reflects the self-reliance and positive spirit she developed after nearly having drowned at sea: "Although there is nothing worse than to confront death, I realized that God gave me a second opportunity, and I was committed to overcoming whatever fear cropped up in my life." Using her creative spirit, Martha translated her experiences of living in two very different worlds in Colombia—the underprivileged world of the students at the school her parents ran, and the upper middle class world she lived in—into a socially relevant cartoon strip. Her parents were the owners of a school that educated the children of chauffeurs, maintenance people, and others at the lower end of the economic ladder. Many of these girls and boys went to school without breakfast, their mothers sometimes going hungry in order to pay for the tuition. Within these families such problems as teen pregnancy and domestic abuse were not uncommon. Touched by their hardships and determination, Martha created cartoon characters based on these children's struggles, as well as on characters reflecting the country club set that inhabits the other end of the economic spectrum.

When I asked her how she got started as a cartoonist Martha told me she had actually begun *Los Kitos* when she was eight years old. "There was a class in my Catholic school on *Papal Encyclical,* where we studied world politics. It was a very boring class for me, but each week I would draw a cartoon character based on the particular subject we were studying. If we were talking about poverty, for example, I would draw a sad character. So with one character per lecture, after a while I had developed a total of two hundred characters." When she was around fifteen Martha put together her first comic strip and circulated it among her classmates, friends, and family. It eventually became the *Los Kitos* strip that now appears in numerous newspapers around the world.

In addition to the storm that transformed and motivated her to turn her cartoon characters into a viable career, Martha also credits her mom. She was the first to show Martha that a creative touch can make every activity more meaningful—and more fun. Using the philosophy that kids should learn through playing, she offered her children creative opportunities at every turn. For example, if Martha had a history test, her mom would make her a Napoleon hat and tell her to put it on and act like Napoleon, to consider what he would have done in a certain situation. The high value Martha's mother placed on creativity would have a tremendous impact on Martha.

Using her artistic skills and her creative spirit, Martha produced a cartoon strip that reflects both her personal emotions and the Latino community she embraces. For this reason *Los Kitos* enjoys a uniquely compelling place in the cartoon world. A cartoon's ability to capture the flavor of a particular culture is something Martha has long been aware of. "Ever since I was very young I recognized how a cartoon shows you a culture. Snoopy, for example, is baseball, football, very all-American. Mickey Mouse resembles the Anglo-Saxon culture—a very disciplined world, very coordinated, very systematized. I wanted to get into cartoons because I had never seen any that projected the Latin American culture. In my cartoons there's soccer, rhythm, fruits, the sun—and the Kitos are very family oriented, very loyal, *pachangueros*. They enjoy dancing and friendship, but they respect the intimate life of the family."

Martha says that women in Latin America are very creative in general—it's something that is simply part of their emotional life. And so she comes by her *espíritu creativo* naturally. "I use my emotional life in my work," she emphasizes. "If I wake up happy, I do cartoons that are very happy. If I wake up sad, I do cartoons that are very sad. And because my cartoons express that emotionality as well as the colorful and rhythmic culture I come from, I see everything more artistically—and with more *sabor*."

Having learned about self-reliance in a crisis that nearly claimed her life, and using that lesson to fuel her creative drive, Martha made her artistic vision a reality. She never allowed fear to block her path. Sometimes fear interferes with our ability to be creative, whether it's fear of the unknown, fear of being criticized, or fear of being seen as "different" to others. When fear stifles our creative spirit we miss out on so many wonderful possibilities. Martha's story inspires all of us to follow through courageously with the dreams our *espíritu creativo* awakens in us.

A Creative Blend of Cultures

Creativity is intrinsic to all human beings, but as we're discovering, Latinas are particularly fortunate in that we tend to have a highly developed creative spirit due to the circumstances we have been called upon to deal with. "Necessity is the mother of invention," Plato reminded us, and throughout our history it has been necessary for us to tap into our creativity and invent new tactics in order to overcome a range of *obstáculos*.

There is also another reason, mentioned in Chapter One, why Latinos in general intrinsically possess a creative perspective: Most of them represent the joining of Indian and European cultures. When the Spaniards conquered Mexico and Central and South America, their dream was to "legitimize" the indigenous people they had overcome by not only making them Christians but also by converting them to their philosophical values and way of life. And the Indians brought to this unsolicited union centuries of sophisticated culture that emphasized loyalty to their gods and harmony with nature. A potent example of this blending of cultures is the dark-skinned Virgin of Guadalupe, who originated in 1531 as a vision seen by a newly converted Indian at the exact location where a shrine to the Aztec goddess Tonantzin (the Mother of Gods) had once been.

Most Latinos—80 percent of whom are *mestizos*—have these two strains, European and Indian, within them, and are therefore predisposed to drawing from more than one cultural resource. Being of two cultures, a blend of both, you have a wider perspective, more choices, and more possibilities. This is also true of others in the United States who are originally from different cultures, and it certainly applies to children of intermarriages. Having at least two different cultural perspectives enhances their sense of creative adaptability. Given that most Latinos personify the blending of two distinct traditions, and that Latinas are the ones in charge of transmitting culture, mores, and values to their children, a spirit of adaptability and creativity is the natural out-come.

You don't have to be a *mestiza* to have this spirit alive within you; however, the creative way in which the women in our communities adapt to new circumstances and challenges is something by which we all are influenced and from which we all learn.

Silvia Bolaños:
Spreading Her Creative Vision

Silvia Bolaños, national sales director for the cosmetics firm Yves Rocher, embodies this union of cultures we've been talking about, and she attributes her success in part to the creative spark she believes results from this combination. Her mother came from Spain and her father from Mexico. Their attitudes and predilections were dissimilar but complementary, and Silvia was inspired by both of them—as well as by her grandmother. When Silvia's maternal grandmother first arrived by herself in Mexico from Spain, she earned a living selling movie tickets, doing what she needed to do to fulfill her dream: becoming a chemist. Silvia's grandmother not only became the head of the laboratory at the department of chemistry for the military hospital in Mexico City, but she always took into her home two or three women who were in need, helping them to overcome whatever difficulties they had. Silvia witnessed all of this. "When my grandmother died, I was surrounded by a lot of women who had been inspired by her. And I, too, saw her as a role model. Although she came to Mexico without a penny, she ended up making a lot of money."

Silvia's mother, who also came originally from Spain, married a man from Veracruz. He was, according to Silvia, an *hombre simpático*. "I was inspired by the strength of my mother and the *simpatía de mi padre,* which molded my personality. I took from my father the ability to be positive and enjoy every single moment. He would say 'We have to live for today,' and my mother would answer 'Yes, but what if you *do* live tomorrow?' So I learned that you have to live for today, tomorrow, and the following day. I realized it was important to enjoy life, but to also keep building toward something every day of your life."

Using a creative combination of traits she was raised with Silvia learned to be creative with her career goals. The blending of cultures she was nourished by and the notions her parents instilled in her of living for today, tomorrow, and the future enabled her to develop a business not just for herself but from which other women also could benefit. Her creative vision, along with the audaciousness to carry it out (which is closely related to the *atrevida* we will be discussing in an upcoming chapter) led her to take up the challenge of moving to a new country and offering exciting new business opportunities to other Latinas.

"I am a very *audaz* woman, and I love to create challenges for myself," Silvia told me. The biggest challenge in her life was to leave Mexico and come to live in the United States. Crossing that border meant changing her life and leaving her country—but it also meant fulfilling a vision she had of helping not only herself but other women. She had been working with the Yves Rocher company in Mexico, and the general director there proposed that she come to the States to open up a branch of their company. Silvia accepted the challenge so that she could work with Latinas in the United States. She says that, although Latinas often are afraid of going out and selling, "I teach them that from the moment you're born you sell yourself in different ways. Even as a child, when you want a candy, you look at your parents with a smile. So you are selling yourself, asking for what you want. I teach women to go for what they want with this premise: I want it, I can do it, and I'm going to get it."

Silvia has opened the market for Yves Rocher in a number of states in the United States, putting ads in local papers and inviting women to cafés to discuss the opportunities to become involved in the cosmetics company she believes in. She also has had tremendous success in Puerto Rico, which is now first in sales, and has been invited by the president of Santo Domingo to bring the business there as well. Silvia has helped more than forty thousand women to become free by having a job that can provide them with economic security. "The most important part of my career is to fight for women to have a place in the world, because when you are born you are 'the daughter of,' when you get married, you are 'the wife of,' and when you have children you are 'the mother of.' But women also have to have their own place to be themselves. I appreciate the chance to offer other women direction — so they can become themselves."

As we'll be discovering throughout the book, the power of one Latina's success story lies in its ability to inspire and build confidence in others. In Silvia's case her *espíritu creativo* helps her to actively seek out women who she knows are in need of the economic and psychological boost afforded them by a career with a company like hers. She is audaciously committed to spreading the sense of pride and fulfillment that develops when a woman becomes her own person and makes her distinctive mark on the outside world.

Demasiado Creativa o no lo Suficiente
Can You Be Too Creative? Not Creative Enough?

There is no such thing as being too creative as you engage in the process of envisioning your future. Even though your dreams may not materialize exactly as you hoped they might, envisioning gives you an overall sense of what you want to fulfill in your life. Still, although creativity is precious and important, so is action. When we have received our "creative flash" and are at the planning stage, we have to remember to get input and advice from those with appropriate experience and to map out the practical steps we'll need to take to get from here to there. The right balance between creativity and common sense is crucial if we are to transform our vision into reality.

When you are estranged from your *espíritu creativo*, on the other

hand, you become stuck in routines and unable to imagine new possibilities. Those who are their own harshest critics—negating a new idea
before it even has a chance to be born—or those who have a hard time
letting go of schedules and perfectionism are the people who have difficulty unleashing their creative spirit. You need to be relaxed and
open—even loose—for ideas and dreams to flow through you. If you
are set in your ways or have a tendency to let your life go on as it always has, be conscious of that. For your *espíritu creativo* to inspire you,
you must be willing to shake things up, to loosen your routine, to let
your uncensored ideas flow in—however wild or unusual they might
seem. There will be a time to fine-tune your creative ideas later, but if
you don't allow them to enter at all, you run the risk of severely limiting your Latina powers.

Exercise: Checking in With Your Childlike Curiosity

Creativity is a natural human condition with which we tend to lose
touch as we get older. Our playfulness, curiosity, and freedom of spirit
often diminish as we are called upon to attend to the practical matters of adulthood. Also, as Latinas, our curiosity can be inhibited by
restrictions—self-imposed, society imposed, family imposed. One way
to get in touch with your *espíritu creativo* is to free yourself from those
restrictions and reconnect with the child you used to be—or the one
you never got a chance to be!

This exercise draws its inspiration from the work of María
Montessori, a nineteenth-century Italian educator who created a theory of education based on the curiosity of the child. Montessori believed that children should be free to explore what interests them and
to discover things for themselves. They learn, she taught, by being in
an environment that offers engaging and stimulating activities from
which they are free to choose.

We can create such an inspiring environment for ourselves and thereby tap into our own curiosity, which in turn will ignite our creative spirit and help us design a life for ourselves that fits who we are. Here are the steps to this exercise:

1. *Promise yourself that you will discover something new every day.*
   Remember the first time you encountered a snake? A rainbow? A train? Snow? Childhood is filled with "firsts," but we don't have to abandon our search for new experiences. Shake up your routine and discover things you've never seen before!
2. *Let your joy and your excitement become your motivation.*
   Can you recall the joyful feeling you had as a little girl when you sailed across the monkey bars on the playground or finger-painted with all your favorite colors? Pay attention to what gives you a thrill, what you're touched by spiritually, emotionally, or intellectually. Follow that feeling—and find out more about that subject, that activity, that thing that fascinates you.
3. *Observe yourself in this free environment.*
   Do you remember watching yourself in the merry-go-round mirror, how thrilled your five-year-old face looked as you magically galloped atop a huge, painted horse? Write down what you have discovered, what has inspired you, what you're feeling excited by. Read it the next day, and a week later, to reassess your feelings.

Remember how curious we were as little girls? We can go back to that spirit of openness, of observing and learning from everything around us. And when we do we'll begin to reach a deeper understanding of who we are—and what new path we want to take. There is no such thing as one "right" way. There are many ways, and we can discover the ones that are most authentically ours by developing the curiosity and intuition we have always possessed.

3

The *Aguantadora's* Passionate Determination

Exile and loneliness—I don't wish that experience on anyone . . .
I think my belief in human beings, in the dignity of humankind, was
what gave me strength. That and my passion for singing!
— Mercedes Sosa, singer

Determination and hard work, even in the direst circumstances, are
not exclusive to the Latino culture. But throughout history Latinos'
ability to embody these core values has been rigorously tested, and
they have always responded with resiliency. Latinos have continued to
move forward in the face of adversity, which has included the Spanish
conquistadors, political and economic instability, uprooting, racism,
sexism, discrimination, and poverty. As Latinas many of us have also
had to endure *machismo* within our communities and families as well as
a patriarchal culture that often restricts us from setting our own goals
and living the lives we would choose for ourselves.

There are also those among us who have had to go through the
tragedy of domestic abuse. According to the U.S. Department of
Justice's National Violence Against Women Survey published in 1998,
approximately 1.5 million women are raped and/or physically assaulted by an intimate partner annually in the United States. In Latin
America, between 10 percent and 30 percent of adult women with
partners suffer physical abuse at the hands of their partners, according
to a study published by the Inter-American Development Bank and
Johns Hopkins University Press. And some studies cite even higher

percentages in particular communities. The Instituto Mexicano de In-
vestigación de la Familia y la Población and the Universidad Autó-
noma de México found that 57 percent of women in Jalisco, México,
and 61 percent in San Miguel de Allende, México, are victims of domestic violence. Sadly, many women who are victims of such abuse
have learned to accept violence, having been physically abused by
their parents. Yet many of those who have dealt with this family horror
have remained strong, even though ultimately they have had to face
the upheaval of leaving an abusive relationship. They have done so in
order to protect their children and advance their own lives.

So, with all—or even some—of these experiences in our background, we have had to hone our *aguantadora* survival skills.

The concept of the *aguantadora* is so strictly a Latina notion that
there is not even an accurate way to translate it into English. It's a mix
of being resilient and persistent. Resilient in the sense that we bounce
back and repair ourselves after withstanding hardship. Persistent in
the sense that we don't let those hardships keep us from doing whatever we set out to do. An *aguantadora* is someone who puts up with "it"
and keeps going—"it" being whatever life throws our way. You take it,
and you take it, and yet you don't allow yourself to be defeated; you
stick to your path. Whatever happens to you, you keep going. You
don't question why things don't go your way, you don't whine or com-
plain or give up—you just keep enduring difficulties and moving on.
You survive.

Today, in our drive to do more than just survive—to discover and
enjoy a fulfilling life, including a possible career outside the home—we
Latinas add something incalculable to our sense of endurance and
commitment: passion! In this chapter we are going to give the familiar
phrase *"Aguántate, mujer"* ("Endure, woman") a new meaning. It will
no longer signify to you that a woman ought to stoically survive her
difficult lot in life; instead, it will take on a radical new significance:
that, as Latinas pursuing our goals, we can employ our natural tenacity
and our unstoppable passion—and go for it!

Through the inspiring stories of Latinas' resilience, persistence, and determination in this chapter, we will witness how women in our culture learn the value of hard work and resolve from their communities or their families and then become *aguantadoras* in their own quest for success in their chosen fields.

The *Aguantadora's* Inheritance
Aztec, Inca, Mestizo, and Spanish Roots

As we mentioned in the first chapter, the roots of an *aguantadora*'s ability to withstand hardship can be traced by some Latinas to the Aztec codices. These codes reflected the Aztecs' vision of their ideal society and included advice to parents about how to bring up their daughters. In addition to honesty, piety, diligence, chastity, obedience, modesty, and mastery of female duties, tenacity in enduring life's difficulties or *tenacidad de aguantar las dificultades de la vida* is listed in the codices as one of the fundamental virtues that parents ought to instill in girls. Of course, our perspective on ideal female virtues has changed over the last five hundred years, but certainly the ability to be tenacious in the face of life's struggles remains a powerfully important attribute.

The history of the Inca women in colonial Peru reveals another aspect of the *aguantadora*'s roots: a courageous determination to preserve her traditions and beliefs. In her book *Moon, Sun and Witches* (Princeton University Press, 1987) anthropologist Irene Silverblatt tells how bravely the indigenous women of Peru resisted the Spaniards who tried to force the Inca people to give up their religious customs and values in favor of Spanish culture and oppressive economic policies. Rather than give in to the Spaniards by becoming *yanaconas* (quasi serfs), as many native men did, these women fled to remote areas where they could practice their native religion and resume the social relations inherent in their culture. They disobeyed the Spanish administrators, the clergy, and their own community officials in order to assure that their culture endured.

The word *aguantar* also has its roots in Spanish culture, as Earl Shorris points out in his book *Latinos: Biography of the People:* "In the lexicon of the bullfight, *aguantar* means to stand firm. . . . '*Aguantar la vara como venga*' means to bear whatever comes, as the bull must bear the *vara* used by the *picador.*" Shorris goes on to say that the Mexican *mestizo* meaning of *aguantar* combines the Spanish notion of enduring danger and suffering and the Indian notion of fatalism and acquiescence to nature, resulting in this definition: "enduring one's fate bravely and with a certain style."

We are going to *aguantar* bravely and with style—but, in harmony with our own nature and by respecting ourselves, we also are going to create our own destiny.

The Fortitude of an Artist
Esperanza Martínez

Perhaps no story epitomizes the passionate *aguantadora* as poignantly as Esperanza Martínez's. She refused to be beaten down by the hard hand life had dealt her, and instead continued throughout her sixty-four years to honor and nourish her talent and her unwavering love for art. She overcame a life of severe hardship, abuse, and sexism to become one of Diego Rivera's few private students, and later a highly respected artist whose work was shown in prestigious museums around the world and purchased for more than $10,000 by such prominent figures as Jacqueline Onassis. Esperanza's vibrant, stirring paintings pay homage to Mexican history and the simple beauties of life in Chiapas and Oaxaca, in the south of Mexico. Esperanza passed away in 1998, and I treasure the intimate moments of conversation and laughter that I shared with her.

It was a miracle that Esperanza even survived her childhood. Born into extreme poverty in Mexico, she grew up in a family where there was never enough to eat and the males always were fed first. When she was eight years old, her grandmother died, leaving Esperanza to assume her role in the family, doing much of the housework and helping her mother to raise the children. By the time she was twelve, four of her younger brothers and sisters had died of malnutrition, largely due to the economic depression in Mexico at the time.

It wasn't only poverty that Esperanza had to contend with as a child, however. Both of her parents were unsupportive and abusive. Still, at an early age, Esperanza discovered she had the desire to be an artist. And she let that desire lead her to those people who would support her lifetime commitment to art. She told me that her grandfather was the one who introduced her to the pencil when she was only three years old, and from her first mark on paper, she delighted in drawing: "My grandfather would take me to his room and give me drawing classes. Although he gave me his approval, he was not very expressive. But he did tell my father that I had talent."

As she got a little older and wanted to learn to paint, Esperanza used her *aguantadora* determination to find a way. With no money to buy art supplies, she actually took hair from the street dogs around her home, taped it to sticks, and made her own paintbrushes. For paint she would obtain colors from stones and grind them to create powder. Then, without her parents knowing, she found someone to teach her how to paint. "I was sabotaged by my parents, not encouraged at all," Esperanza told me. "Both of my parents were abusive, but I found a way to learn. I had a teacher from the age of seven and was fascinated to go to my teacher's studio. Just the experience of smelling the paints inspired me."

When she was twelve Esperanza sold her first painting. She continued to study and learn and paint. Unable to rely on her family for encouragement or validation, she actively sought out teachers and mentors who showed her the way as an artist. She spoke appreciatively of these people and credited them with strengthening her faith in herself as an artist: "One important teacher didn't even charge me for teaching me. He gave me the materials for my classes and made the contact with my first agent. He was like a grandfather, who could understand my problems at that time. And there was a friend, a pioneer, a world prestigious artist who influenced my choice in themes for my paintings. I admired many other painters, but that man had an immense influence on my life, both personally and artistically."

With all the economic hardship and family abuse she had to endure, Esperanza never allowed the potentially devastating problems life presented her with to blur the focus on her unending mission: to express the beauty and truth of her people, their customs, their way of life, and the history that they embodied. Although female artists were largely ignored in Mexico during the 1930s and 1940s when she was growing up and beginning her career, Esperanza didn't let that hold her back either. When her parents expressed their opinion that the successful artist Frida Kahlo was nothing more than a "loose woman," Esperanza refused to let their sexist negativity crush her dream of becoming an accomplished, professional painter. In order to pay for classes at the Academia de San Carlos in Mexico City, she worked at two jobs and sold her paintings as well. It was at the *academia* that she met the world famous artist Diego Rivera, who took her under his wing as one of his few private pupils.

Esperanza never relented in her commitment to grow as an artist. Even in her early sixties, when I asked her how her artistic output had changed over the years, she told me, "Changes are happening now. I am still completely and fully dedicated to my love — painting." Esperanza created her paintings with an abiding passion, using everything that she had, as well as all she had been deprived of. Art was not only her contribution to the Mexican people she loved, it was also her most deeply felt desire.

This talented person, whose dynamic, haunting paintings hang in my home and in museums throughout the world, gave us a profoundly meaningful message in the way she got through the harsh circumstances of her life: *Aguántate, mujer.* Endure the hardships by carving out your own gratifying and joy-filled path. Live well, despite your past sorrows. Allow yourself to have another kind of life than the one you were born into. Create the existence you want for yourself.

Even when we don't have role models in our family, we need to be able to retreat from blaming and fault finding in others and in society. We can't get stuck in the idea that "I was raised in this way, so I can't do this or I can't achieve that." We cannot keep blaming others or society, or the church, or anything else in our background. It's within our power to make changes.

Esperanza's paintings are proof that when you are a true *aguantadora*, even the most dreadful circumstances cannot extinguish the spark of passion that each of us is born with. Our dedication and eagerness can prevail, helping us to succeed. And keeping at it, in the face of even overwhelming difficulties, will give us the self-respect and the pride that develop when we're tested in this way. Perhaps we doubt that we have the strength required to endure. *The strength comes by doing it.* We can't measure how strong we are *before* taking on the challenge of changing our lives. We must make the changes by *doing it*, and in the process we become strong.

Still, it's important to realize that not many women become strong by themselves. Usually there is a strong mother or a strong grandmother—or in Esperanza's case a supportive grandfather and teacher—who inspire and encourage us, as the stories throughout this book reveal. But if we're not fortunate enough to have such guiding forces in our lives, we can create an inspiring force within ourselves. At times we may feel vulnerable and we may believe that we can't keep going. That sense of insecurity is a common response. On our path through life we will question ourselves many, many times, wondering if we're going to fail. Confronting those feelings and still progressing forward is what will give us the *aguantadora's* strength that we need to keep going.

Being an *aguantadora* means that we have the determination to be who we are meant to be, to prevail. We will make this happen in a very realistic way. Whatever our goals are, we can learn to ask ourselves the probing questions and give ourselves honest answers. Esperanza knew she was born to be an artist. That didn't mean, however, that she didn't need to find a teacher, many teachers, and to learn by making mistakes along the way. It's very important at this *aguantadora* stage of our journey that we be honest and realistic about our abilities and goals so that our passion and determination are grounded in what is authentically possible.

Overcoming an Environment of Poverty and Violence
Dr. Estela Martínez

Growing up in West Fresno, California, a very poor, African-American and Latino community, Estela Martínez was forced to become an *aguantadora* in order to pursue her dreams. Most of the families in her neighborhood lived in the government housing projects, as hers did, and received subsidized income from the state, as her family did off and on. There were no Latino or African-American teachers in her elementary school.

How did Estela acquire the determination to become a doctor and to go after the education she needed when those around her were falling prey to the dangers inherent in deprived neighborhoods? Her earliest influence was her mother, who valued education even though she had none herself. She never missed an opportunity to tell her seven sons and five daughters that they would do well in life if they were well educated. "While other Latino girls were raised to learn cooking and cleaning and child care," Estela told me, "my mother worked very hard so that I wouldn't have to do any of the house chores. What I did have to do was work hard at school and complete my homework conscientiously. My mother would tell me, 'I will take care of your father, cook, clean, do his shirts—everything for him. But you are not going to do that. You are not going to grow up simply to be of service to your husband.' I listened to my mother and believed her."

Today Estela admits that she sees nothing inherently wrong in doing domestic chores ("If they're done out of love, but not exclusively.") and that even back then they would not have kept her from studying. She loved the adventure of learning, and nothing would have stood in the way of chasing after it. What she wasn't always aware of, though, was how bright she really was. "I learned that I was smart when I was in fourth grade," she told me. "Before that, I didn't know if I was. In fourth grade I got an academic award signifying that I was at the top of my class. It came as a total surprise to me—and it surprised my family when I brought the award home. My mother asked my father, 'Didn't you notice that she was getting straight As?' Apparently he hadn't. But when somebody points out to you that you are excelling it makes you want to continue to do well. I was always competing with these two Chinese guys who were very good students, always had the best grades. So when I won the award, I told myself, 'Hey, I'm even better than these two guys!' And that raised my competitiveness within myself."

Estela's early academic triumph was no guarantee of her future success. In fact, when she reached junior high, her path was thwarted by a sexist counselor and a violent campus environment. Her *aguantadora* spirit already was being challenged. In seventh grade she wanted to take music as an elective, but the counselor told her, "Oh, no, no, no. Girls have to take home economics, because you are going to grow up to be a mommy." Although she felt the sting of a male counselor who didn't respect her, Estela enrolled in home economics—and never took music. "I was shy at that time, and easily intimidated," she confessed. "My mother was a little bit offended by the advice the counselor gave me, but she was intimidated too."

Estela continued to attend that particular junior high school, but did so in fear. It was a hostile atmosphere, with more than its share of violence and crime. It turns out that the kids who were the greatest source of her fear were well known in the neighborhood. But a few of them had not always been associated with trouble, and their transformation from decent kids into troublemakers made a big impression on Estela: "There was one family in my neighborhood that had a big impact on me because they made me realize how much your environment can change you. It was an African-American family, a single mother with two children. The mom had initially enrolled the kids in Catholic school, and at that time they were clean-cut, smart, good kids. But then they were transferred to public school, and they were utterly transformed—smoking in the bathrooms, drinking, chasing after girls—always getting into trouble. Their mother didn't know what to do."

Not wanting to offend these particular neighbors, Estela accepted their invitation to attend a party at their house—but was extremely frightened by what happened there. "In our neighborhood, African Americans were not proud to be African American, and Latinos weren't proud to be Latino either. And the African-American kids were confused about me, because I am very *morena,* but I have straight hair. I look black, but I'm not. So at this party they wanted to beat me up because of the way I looked—not black but not white either. They threatened me just for that reason."

Finally, one day after school Estela came home and told her mom, "If you don't let me transfer, I'm going to die here." She was thirteen years old. A week before, a guy had put a knife to her stomach and threatened her sexually. She managed to get away from him and run home, but she was so traumatized by the event that when she asked her mom if she could transfer to another school, Estela already had worked out a plan: "I had it all figured out. I could take the bus downtown and then take another bus to the other junior high school. It meant forty-five minutes travel time, but I had to take the ball and run with it. I pleaded with my mom, made my case, and she agreed."

Being the determined and resourceful *aguantadora* that she was, even at the age of thirteen, Estela made the transfer to the safer school on the other side of town. This school also had some excellent women teachers, who provided crucial role models for Estela at this important time in her life. They were young, they were smart, they were involving, and Estela had the feeling, because these were young females, that if they could make something of their lives, she could too. She especially was impressed by her geometry teacher, who was pregnant with her fourth child. "She was very smart, and an example of how you could be a wonderful teacher at the same time as being a mother, pregnant, and a wife. She was a big inspiration to me."

In high school Estela realized she was good in science and math and started to make plans for college and her eventual career. Like many Latinas, she wanted to be involved in a service-oriented career, but at the same time be creative and be a leader. So she had to make a decision concerning what she would do within the field of science. She decided to be a doctor rather than a nurse because, in her research at the high school career center, she found out that doctors and nurses take a similar course of study, except that doctors are in school for more years, which she had no problem with.

At this point in her life Estela met the person who would help her follow the path she had set early on as a determined *aguantadora*. Her mother had provided her with the belief in education and in sticking to your goals; her female teachers had provided inspiration; and now another important influence would provide the reinforcement and guidance so vital to Latinas from backgrounds similar to Estela's. She told me about an important man in her life named Roberto Ruvalcaba. "This wonderful person entered my life," she recalled. "He was the Equal Opportunity Program (EOP) director at the University of California, Santa Cruz, and he came to our high school to recruit students. He wanted to see the records of all the Latino students who were doing well. So he called us in, one by one, and told us about the program at Santa Cruz and then asked us what our plans were. Other students were saying things like, 'Oh, I want to be a legal secretary,' but five minutes after talking to Mr. Ruvalcaba, they wanted to be a lawyer. Or if a boy said he wanted to be a dental hygienist, five minutes later, after

Mr. Ruvalcaba's input, that boy wanted to be a dentist. When it was my turn I said, 'I want to be a doctor,' and Mr. Ruvalcaba beamed back at me and said, 'Wonderful!' "

Thanks to Mr. Ruvalcaba, Estela entered an intense seven-week college prep program for disadvantaged students that helped them with the more difficult classes they needed to get into college. Estela learned trigonometry and calculus and was introduced to advisers who later helped her get accepted into medical school. "There were eight of us in the program, and the teachers affirmed my goals and determination, because they kept telling me, 'You're doing well and you're going to make it,' even though at that point I was just graduating from high school."

Estela—now Dr. Estela Martínez, anesthesiologist, wife, and mother of three-and-a-half-year-old twins—had a lot of obstacles: coming from a poor neighborhood in which very few people valued education; having to put up with a violent school environment; struggling against racist and sexist attitudes. "But what helped me through it," she confirms, "was being raised by my mother, who kept telling me, 'You are different. You can do it. You can get an education and have a good career.' "

Estela's mom also put her foot down—perhaps a bit harshly by today's standards, but effectively nonetheless—when it came to Estela's social life. She would tell Estela, "No boyfriends! If you get a boyfriend, before you know it you are pregnant, and then your highest aspiration will be to buy a car, and then you will have to work at a low-paying job just to pay for the car." Consequently, Estela wasn't very involved socially, because she felt it would take too much time and energy away from school: "I put myself above the other girls and found myself a different peer group—guys. Because they were the ones who were working hard to excel academically. When you surround yourself with people who have the same goals as you do, it molds you. I could call these friends in the middle of the night and ask them a trigonometry question, and they were always available to me."

Because of Estela's positive experience at the cross-town junior high school and high school, her younger siblings also eventually attended the schools, even though it meant the inconvenience of traveling a considerable distance from their home. Of those siblings, one brother became an environmental engineer, another a writer (and recipient of the 1998 National Book Award for his novel, *A Parrot in the Oven*), another works at a law firm, another has a degree in psychology and works with disabled children, and another is an artist. As for her sisters, one became a teacher and the other, "a casualty of being a Latina," says Estela, got pregnant when she was a teenager and became a homemaker. Although this sister doesn't feel confident enough to continue with an education, she successfully raised two girls who are both in college. Estela's older siblings, who didn't attend the better junior high and high school, have good lives but became employees, not professionals, because they didn't have access to higher education.

In summing up her *aguantadora* determination, Estela told me, "It takes a lot of strength to keep pushing ahead when you're up against the kind of problems my community was faced with. I don't know where I got it. Probably from my grandfather, who struggled so hard to learn English. When I went to elementary school, he went to school too—adult school. And I thought, Great! We're going to go to school together. I spent a lot of time at his house, and I would wake up late at night and see him still studying. He would ask me questions about what he was studying, and even if I hadn't learned it yet, I would try to figure it out and explain it to him. I saw the patience my grandfather had, struggling to become more educated at his age. And I thought, 'Hey, if he can do that, I can do this too.' "

Estela was wise enough to look around her and see what was happening in her community and to make certain that she avoided the kind of mistakes too many disadvantaged children make. She acknowledged the disadvantages but created a plan for breaking out of the cycle of poverty. And she stuck to it (*aguántate, mujer!*), even when it seemed that so many daunting circumstances were conspiring against her.

Like Estela, we can keep our eyes open and make the decisions that will enhance our futures. Even if you are in the worst of environments, you can still be faithful to yourself and to your goals—and prevail. You can tell yourself, as Estela's mother repeated so often to her, "You are different—you can make it."

Gaining Resilience from Doing What You Love
Singer Mercedes Sosa

Born in Tucumán, in the north of Argentina, Mercedes Sosa is well known throughout Latin America and the world for her deep, expressive voice that can transform a song into a mesmerizing and unforgettable personal message. Mercedes's wonderful voice seems to erupt directly from the earth, like a volcano. She was one of the originators of Latin America's *"nueva canción"* movement of the sixties, and she has used her warm contralto voice to urge political reform and democracy, referring to her songs as *"canciones de barricadas."* In the late 1970s the repressive military regime in Argentina outlawed her concerts and banned her recordings, and in 1979 forced Mercedes into exile due to what they perceived as the subversiveness of the songs she sang. Recalling what it felt like to be prevented from doing what she most loved, and then to be expelled from her country and estranged from her family and friends, Mercedes still shudders to think of what she went through then: "The military were watching me. They prohibited me from singing because they thought I was a *guerrillera*. They didn't let me sing! The songs were just folk songs, many from Chile because I sang those of the Chilean songwriter Violeta Parra. Exile and loneliness—I don't wish that experience on anyone. It was a four-year exile, and it was *haaard.*" Mercedes's husband had died already, but her son, Fabian, came with her to Paris, where she rented an apartment. And then her son had to go back to Argentina: "Can you imagine how it was for me when Fabian left? I was heartbroken, by myself, totally alone."

When an *aguantadora* is faced with a crisis, it isn't that she doesn't feel the pain or the heartbreak of the experience; what defines her as someone whom we admire and learn from is her ability to be resilient, to remain focused on her calling and dedicated to her mission. Mercedes Sosa knew then, as she does now, that she was born to sing. Her purpose in life is to inspire people with her evocative voice and meaningful songs. And she takes great pleasure in doing this, as we all take pleasure in accomplishing those things that represent the deepest part of ourselves. When I asked her what inner resources she called upon to be able to survive being in exile, she replied, "Singing! I always have strength when I sing, and always singing makes me feel good. I was making very little money in Europe, but I worked a lot, and the love and affection from people was very beautiful. I had the opportunity to meet people, to make friends, and I never felt abandoned because the public never abandoned me."

A worse experience than being exiled from her country was the loss of her beloved husband, Pancho, who had died from a brain tumor the year before Mercedes left Argentina. Losing him and learning to live without the man she loved, she said, was "the hardest thing in my life." But she called upon her *aguantadora*'s resilience at that time, too. She suffered greatly, but at the same time was able to feel that her life had been blessed by her marriage to Pancho. "My husband was my beautiful, super companion. He was such a marvelous man. It's very hard to find someone like that, and I was very blessed to have a companion like he was. Even today I still ask, 'Why do we have to lose someone we love so much?' But we can't always have what we love for our whole lives."

What Mercedes continues to enjoy, however, is her love of singing. When you have a genuine passion for what you're doing, it helps you get through painful events in your life because your heart is in that activity, whatever it might be. And with a connection to your heart, you gain resilience and hope. For Mercedes that way of connecting is through her songs. She sends love to those who hear her, and many more people than she imagines love her back. When we share our talents and passion with others, it generates love. Which always helps us to *aguantar.*

When an *Aguantadora's* Dream Conflicts with Her Family's
Dr. Mary López

Like Estela Martínez, Mary López was determined to get a university education, regardless of the stumbling blocks, so that she could become a professional and pursue the goals she envisioned for herself. In her case, however, her love for and loyalty to her family—which we all share as Latinas—were at odds with her *aguantadora's* commitment to her goals.

Mary's parents wanted only the best for their children. Her father had moved the family from Mexico to Oakland, California, in the hopes of making a better life. When he saw the dangers that poor families in Oakland were exposed to, however, he was frightened for his children. Drugs, crime, a lack of hope or direction—this was not what he wanted for his family. So while he remained in Oakland to earn a living, his wife and six children returned to Mexico.

As a young girl in Mexico, Mary had the good fortune to have a mom who believed in her and encouraged her to plan for a worthwhile career. Her mother told all of her children that they were each going to amount to something in life. "Every day she would ask us what we were going to be when we grew up. Even if we changed our ideas about this from one day to the next, we always had goals, thanks to mom. And I always knew that I was going to go to a university."

Unfortunately, when it was time for her to go to college, Mary was unable to get into the universities in Mexico, due to the fact that she was born in the United States and was therefore a U.S. citizen. For the same reason, though, she was qualified for a university in the States. But there was another major stumbling block: Mary's mother would not allow her to go. Given their bad experiences in Oakland, she was afraid for Mary to go back to the country where there were too many potential dangers. Mary's mom wanted her to stay in Mexico and, since she couldn't get into college, she could become a secretary.

This was simply not acceptable to Mary. She had set her sights on a professional career in the sciences, and she needed a university degree. In order to follow through with her commitment to herself and her dream, she had to make the move to the United States. "Nobody in my family was happy about my going to the States, but I was determined. They thought I would become a drug addict, or a prostitute, or that I would end up being a single mother. But I knew those things wouldn't happen to me," Mary said. She was going to the States with a goal, one she had had since she was a little girl: to go to the university. She knew she would get there, regardless of how. "I wouldn't even look at how; I was only focused on the goal itself. I knew I was going to complete my university degree, no matter what."

The word Mary kept coming back to as she told me about her years at the university was "resiliency." There were many nights when she didn't have the time to sleep, days when she had to work twenty consecutive hours in the lab, months when she had very little money to live on. But her resolve never weakened; she kept her mind focused on the outcome of all her hard work and sacrifices: She would become a scientist. That kind of focused resolve is the essence of the *aguantadora*. But Mary admits that her determination was mixed with remorse. She didn't want to have to leave her family or to disappoint or worry her mother.

"If I had listened to my mom, I wouldn't have left Mexico. I felt guilty for not being with her, and I still feel guilty. Yesterday was my daughter's fourth birthday, and my husband and my daughter and I couldn't celebrate with my family. They still recriminate me, saying, 'You see, if you had stayed here we would all be celebrating together.'

But I know that coming to the States and being away from my family is the price I had to pay for fulfilling my obligation to myself—to become what I was meant to be."

Moving away from a family she cherishes wasn't easy, and there have been times when Mary doubted her *aguantadora*'s strength. She told me that she has been able to endure everything she's been through by having faith in God. Her passionate determination—built on the foundation of her parents' love and encouragement—has kept her fixed on her goals. Still, it is only human to question whether you have made the right choices, especially when they have meant leaving your family of origin. When she feels that the strength she needs to continue on her path is waning, Mary finds that strength in God.

And where did Mary's path ultimately take her? After receiving her bachelor's degree from the University of California at San Diego, she was awarded a Ford Foundation fellowship and went on to earn her Ph.D. in endocrinology. Today she is a professor of endocrinology at Harvard University. Like her mother did with her, Dr. López now asks her four-year-old daughter this question every day: "What do you want to be when you grow up?" And her little girl answers, "A scientist, a teacher, an artist, and a mom." Mary tells her daughter that she's certain she can do all of that.

Only Supportive Relationships Can Support an *Aguantadora*

A mature and supportive relationship—whether it be with a mate, a significant other, or a friend—will be invaluable to you as you practice being a successful *aguantadora* and going after your desired goals. Such a relationship needs to be both nurturing and mutually gratifying. As you're learning to draw upon the inner strength to endure hardships and stay focused on what you want to do, you will need to affirm yourself and your abilities. If you have someone by your side, who will also acknowledge your strengths, offer their counsel when it is helpful, be there for you on the good days and the not so good ones, you have gold in your hands. If you don't have such a person, you can look for positive role models and create that friend within yourself. Remember that you really can be a best friend to yourself. If you know yourself, there's no better ally for you. Still, a constructive relationship with someone else — someone who appreciates the dedication and passion you have for your work — can give you the support to stay focused on what you want to do with your life, especially during times of crisis.

As Latinas, we need to be very aware of our tendency to invest a great deal in our loving relationships, and of the fact that too often we're asked to give up our dreams and hopes for love. When we do this, we cancel out ourselves in favor of pleasing our man. But by canceling out ourselves, we also cancel out our ability to love anyone authentically. You can't be true and loving to someone else by being untrue and unloving to yourself. So if fear of losing someone you love is standing in the way of becoming a successful *aguantadora,* think about whether the loss of yourself is a price you're willing to pay for that relationship.

What are some of the characteristics of a supportive partner? These are the key elements:

- He supports you emotionally—during the good times and bad. (And this means *your* good and bad times, as well as *his.*)
- He doesn't stand in the way of you pursuing the things that bring you fulfillment.
- He encourages you to be the best you can be—and nurtures you as you make strides toward your goals.
- He understands who you are and what you want from life.
- He enjoys your achievements with you.

Aguanta Too Much *y Aguanta* Too Little

When we take *aguantar* to its unhealthy extreme, it can result in our ability to tolerate too much. Of course we want to become resilient enough and strong enough to put up with life's obstacles and challenges. But there is a profound difference between stoically and interminably putting up with a roadblock and bravely putting up with it just long enough to figure out how to get past it. The point is to confront the barriers we come across in life and turn them into stepping stones on the road to our goals.

There are those who endure too much and then blame themselves for not being able to put up with even more hardship than they're already shouldering. This shadow side of the *aguantadora* constantly tells herself, *"Aguántate, como mujer,"* and doesn't know when an unhealthy boundary has been reached. Why are we, as Latinas, especially prone to this type of mind-set?

Our Latino culture is a positive influence in that it values those who uncomplainingly put up with life's difficulties, who endure hardships in pursuit of a worthy goal. But the shadow side of that value is an admiration of those who ceaselessly suffer and make sacrifices without any regard for their own personal goals. If you fall into the latter category, beware. When you are *aguantando* just for its own sake, thinking that at the end of the road you will be acknowledged for all the sacrifices you've made, you are setting yourself up for disappointment, because nobody is likely to give you that acknowledgment. The "pleasers" who sacrifice in this way usually are taken advantage of and end up being unappreciated and depressed.

Also, women who endure the loss of their own dreams, their own lives, by saying "I don't ask for anything; I give because there is pleasure in giving" actually harm those to whom they give so much. Because they make the other person become dependent on them, which is not a healthy relationship for either party. When we *aguantamos* so that we're entirely focused on another person's life, ignoring our own goals, we're not helping the other person; we're interfering. And we're losing ourselves in the process.

On the other hand, when we're unable to deal with virtually any obstacle or hardship on our path toward success, it might mean that we come from a family environment in which everything was done for us. If this is the case, we have been deprived of experiences that are necessary in order to develop an *aguantadora's* resilience. When parents or older siblings always are protecting us from potential dangers, we don't have the opportunities to get knocked down and then to pull ourselves up again. (They don't call the value of such experience "the College of Hard Knocks" for nothing!) So we need to become aware of this lack of experience and take measures to toughen ourselves up. These might include something as simple as a self-encouraging pep talk to stick with a project when we're having a hard time with it, or as challenging as pushing ourselves to try something we want to do but which we've avoided because it won't be easy.

Exercise: Strengthening the *Aguantadora* Within

Sometimes we forget to give ourselves credit for dealing with difficult circumstances. As *aguantadoras* it is very important that we do this so that next time we're faced with an obstacle we know we can count on our own past experiences. A powerful way to ignite your passionate determination is to become inspired by your past triumphs. When you remember how you were able to get through a tough situation, you will be counseling yourself to believe that you can do so once again. We learn who we are, what our strengths are, and how capable we are of doing things we never thought we could when we are tested by hardships. But too often we forget to notice how many of those tests we passed with flying colors. Once you fully acknowledge how much you have overcome in your past, and really feel those triumphs inside you, how they have strengthened you, you will know that there are very few limits on what you are capable of.

This seven-step written exercise will help you get in touch with your personal *aguantadora* history. Notice how recalling a past triumph can inspire you to take on whatever challenge you're currently facing.

1. List specific challenging or difficult events in your life that you confronted successfully. For example, a new job, an exam, moving to a new environment, speaking in public, a financial problem, or an illness. After you have made your list, circle the most significant challenge on the list.

2. List the specific concerns you had as you first confronted the challenge and did not yet know you would succeed. For example, not having someone to rely on, not having sufficient experience, not knowing where to get needed information or advice.

3. Write down what your deepest fears were in confronting that challenge. For example, fear of abandonment, failure, shame, disapproval, physical harm.

4. Write down whether or not these particular fears turned out to have been based on false assumptions and how you discovered this.

5. Write down what you did to be able to succeed in confronting the challenge referred to above. For example, got training or took a class, followed an expert's or a *comadre*'s advice and/or got their moral support, consulted with your intuition, acted as if you were strong (even if you didn't quite believe it) and just did it, believed in your own abilities.

6. Write down what your most important wish was as you attempted to successfully confront that difficult challenge. For example, to be valued, to be heard, to prove that you could do it, to feel smart, to become independent, to be loved, to be financially stable.

7. Write what you learned from successfully confronting the challenge. For example, that you could trust yourself, that you have to pay attention to your own wisdom, that you know the answers if you listen to yourself, that you can ask for assistance when you need it, that you can take on new responsibilities, that you can trust your *aguantadora*'s passionate determination!

As you come to a new path, one that you have chosen yet which elicits troubling thoughts or fears, think about what you have just learned from this exercise. Acknowledge that you have overcome similar fears in the past and allow that knowledge to strengthen you. You have the experience of calling upon your resources and prevailing—and you can do it again. By reconnecting with your strengths you can claim your *aguantadora's* power.

We're On a New Mission

As women we're always taught that we have to *aguantar* because we have to do whatever it takes to give to others — to your father, to your brothers, to your children, to your husband. Many of us still anticipate a life of sacrifice during which we will continually be called upon to *aguantar*. Well, now we're going to change the equation from *aguantártelas* to taking care of ourselves. We're no longer going to be the martyrs, the *sacrificadas*, the *abnegadas*, and all of those things that we were taught we should be proud of being. There's a lot we have to be proud of in our cultural background, but we have to apply our ability to *aguantar* to a much more significant purpose, as we have been describing in this chapter. Our goal is to be resilient, to face the setbacks and barriers and to become an *aguantadora* in an active, positive sense — so that we don't just survive, we become.

When you are a true *aguantadora*, you can *aguantar* everything that life gives you because you approach it as a challenge to an inspiring, fulfilling existence. So, *aguántate, mujer,* and as you consider the pain and frustration and *problemas* that we're each called upon to endure throughout a lifetime, use those experiences. They are your tools, not for staying put, but for heading out to accomplish your new mission in life: becoming yourself.

4

The *Comadre's* Networking Ability

I have always worked with women and for women all my life. And I know how *abnegadas* we women are. I was able to survive the abandonment by my father, being in exile for political reasons, being in poverty, and going through the death of my child—I was able to survive all of that because of my contact with thousands of other women.

— Isabel Allende, writer

The power of women all over the world networking and sharing their ideas ultimately results not only in personal growth but in profound social change. Each of us, whether we fully realize it or not, draws strength from our *comadre* connections. How might these strong ties to other Latinas and other women in general translate into a powerful force that can propel us toward our chosen goals? The word *"comadre"* needs no translation for Latinas, but when I tried to explain it to an Anglo friend I realized there is no similar word in English. "Close friend" or "best friend" are phrases that come the closest, but my non-Spanish-speaking colleague had an interesting thought. She said, "Maybe it means just what it sounds like—a kind of comothering?"

In fact, a *comadre* is someone with whom you enjoy a mutually nurturing relationship, someone whom you may consider a spiritual or honorary family member. When you and another woman are *comadres*, in the way we are now going to define that word, you each take on the role of a caring "comother" who helps to nurture and develop the other's dreams and projects. *Comadres* also take on the roles of sister, ally, *tía*, counselor, cousin, mentor, advocate, confidant—and more. They become someone you can trust forever, unconditionally.

What are some of the core qualities that go into building this relationship so intrinsic to our Latina way of life? Respect, openness, trust, generosity, affection, humor, supportiveness—*y más*. And when such a relationship exists, it can motivate and encourage you, help you handle setbacks, even inspire you to see an expanded vision of yourself. When you are in a *comadre* relationship with another woman or a group of women, you give openly and unselfishly, and you receive what is offered to you with the same openness.

In this chapter we're going to focus on a gift we treasure in our personal friendships but too often neglect in other areas of our life, including our work or profession: our innate skill at being *comadres*. As outward-reaching, supportive *comadres* we've inherited from our Latina culture something we can now use to help us realize our plans and fulfill our aspirations as well as develop our spiritual selves. Many of us take for granted our ability to support each other, but in fact it is one of the most prized strengths in nearly every field of endeavor, including business, politics, and the arts.

As I mentioned in the first chapter, I often think that Latinas were the ones to invent networking, because we are used to connecting with our *comadres* in order to help out each other's families, extend ourselves to neighbors and friends, and improve our communities. When a challenge arises, we put our heads together, pool our talents, and get into action to deal with it. We don't think twice about enlisting each other's help. Our female contacts are essential to us, and we have learned from our culture to value these important relationships. But do we also consider our *comadres* as potential resources that can be used to further each other's personal goals? And do we nourish our female relationships to the extent that we're more attuned to our spiritual selves—and more capable of helping ourselves and others to grow?

Career experts remind us that networking is one of the keys to success. Since Latinas already know how to give to and receive from our *comadres* by forging close ties with one another, we already hold that key.

So now let's find out how other women have parlayed their *comadre* networking skills into the pursuit of their dreams — and how you can too.

Linda Gutiérrez: How Two Women Became Two Thousand

Chair of the board of directors of the National Hispana Leadership Institute, president of the Hispanic Women's Corporation, and member of the Arizona-Mexico Commission Health Committee, the Arizona Children's Action Alliance Advisory Committee, Salud Inc.'s School-Based Clinic Advisory Board, the National Council of La Raza, and Chicanos Por La Causa Advisory Board, Linda Gutiérrez is a doer. "We make things happen because we rely on our energy and our passion," she told me. Linda is dedicated to building an organization that empowers women, and the National Hispana Leadership Institute does that by helping women connect with each other. With each connection, woman by woman, support is given and strengths are developed. The NHLI program mission is "to develop Hispanas as ethical leaders through training, professional development, relationship building and community and world activism."

Linda wasn't born a chairwoman of the board, but she's always had the instincts of an organizer and connecter. She credits her grandmother with showing her how authentic connections are forged and how a true sense of community is created. "I learned how to be a good *comadre* watching my *abuelita*," Linda told me. "She got people together to help build the St. Anthony Church in Phoenix, where she felt most at home after she moved there from Guadalajara. Initially, she had no friends and no immediate family, so, since the church is a natural resource for Latinos, she felt an affinity there. For the next sixty years, she helped the church expand—putting together the church fiestas, doing the *tamaladas*. The events were always successful—and the *tamaladas* were phenomenal! Watching her accomplish all that with her *comadres*, and getting her children and grandchildren involved too, provided me with the stepping stones to successful planning, organizing, and promotion."

Linda also honed her organizational and people skills working in her parents' small store. She learned how to communicate easily with customers while she was cashiering, and being responsible for inventories gave her a crash course in the fundamentals of business. Although as a young teenager she sometimes wondered why she wasn't out playing with the other kids, she admits, "I really learned how to work with customers, be service-oriented, and reach out to people."

Like so many other Latinas I've spoken with, Linda talked of being inspired by her mother's strength in overcoming the many obstacles an immigrant faces. Coming here from Guadalajara as a child, her mom had to struggle because she didn't know the language and always felt that that was a barrier. But it didn't stand in her way. Her children were going to "conquer the world," she used to say. She always told Linda to be an *atrevida* and not be afraid. Try out for sports, try to run for office, do what you have to do—and ask for help if you need it. "I grew up with self-confidence and a belief in myself because my mom gave me a spirit of power," Linda says.

Linda's mother wasn't the only one to offer her an empowering message as well as the affirming encouragement to identify and accomplish her goals. In 1981, she was approached by Nancy Jordan, originally from Sinaloa, Mexico, who asked Linda to become involved in a networking organization for Latinas. Nancy emphasized that she envisioned the organization as a forum where Latinas would learn from each other and develop their professional and leadership potential. She began the organization by calling a small group of women who she knew would be interested in a network of *comadres*, and they in turn phoned those who also were excited about getting the ball rolling, and much to Nancy's delighted surprise, three hundred women showed up at the first meeting. Realizing that this unexpected turnout signaled a real need in the Phoenix community, Nancy enlisted Linda's help in expanding the organization.

"Nancy called me to help her," Linda recalls. "I was expecting my fourth child at the time, and she told me, 'Don't worry. You'll find the time.' I thought maybe I wouldn't be able to do it, but she encouraged me. She turned over the chairmanship to me and told me, 'Dream as big as you want.' I wanted to make it a national organization, and that's what I did." Linda's *comadre* organization has grown to over two thousand women in the last four years. That never could have happened without someone else reaching out to Linda—and Linda in turn reaching out to others.

It doesn't matter what level or stage of life you're at, Linda emphasized, the strengths and support of other women—bolstering your confidence, sharing your vision—can't help but work wonders. Whether you're a student, a secretary, an entrepreneur, or a corporate executive, when you've got another woman's, or many other women's dedication and allegiance behind you, your power is multiplied.

The "Latina Feminist *Testimonios*" Project and Miriam's Daughters

There are thousands of inspiring examples of how *comadre* networking works to make worthwhile things happen in a way that women working alone cannot. The Latina Feminist *Testimonios* project is one such case that serves as a wonderful model. Some of you may have had the experience of being in an academic environment where competitiveness and isolation set the tone among both students and faculty. With so few slots available at the top of any academic ladder, especially at the university level, it's not surprising. So when a group of Latina professors and scholars came together to share their most revealing thoughts and ideas about the Latina experience—and then decided to publish their discoveries—it was noteworthy. They met over a period of seven years, dedicating themselves to the sharing of *testimonios*— stories of their lives. These include autobiographical narratives, short stories, poems, and dialogues. Many of the women involved in this project are professional *testimoniadoras*—oral historians, literary scholars, ethnographers, creative writers, and psychologists. But they never had made their own life trajectories a source of inquiry. Although they were all Latina feminists in higher education, their perspectives spanned a wide range. But with all their differences in national origin, religion, politics, sexual orientation, class background, and academic fields, they employed their essential *comadre* connections to create a book of powerfully honest and diverse personal histories. The creation of *Telling to Live: Latina Feminist Testimonios* by The Latina Feminist Group (Duke University Press, Durham and London, 2001) was built on a foundation of *"comadre*-ship."

In the introduction to their book the authors make the point that by sharing their stories they broke down academic and other barriers and created commonality and empowerment. They are keenly aware that in so doing they were embodying "the Latin American/Latina tradition of kinship, reciprocity, and commitment."

[We] . . . built a sustaining practice of community where we remain committed to continued dialogue, collaboration, and contact, as a whole and in smaller groups. We affirmed a relational ethic of care and support for each other and for the group. In our experience, this is Latina feminism at its most nurturing and creative.

There are many ways that we Latinas are relating to and working with each other to enrich our lives and accomplish our goals. The Latina Feminist *testimonios* created a new way of sharing our stories and letting other people know about our lives. And there are other collections of Latina writings gathered in a similar spirit of *comadre*-ship.

For example, *Miriam's Daughters: Jewish Latin American Women Poets*, edited by Marjorie Agosín (Sherman Asher Publishing, 2001), brings together twenty-eight voices of women who explore their dual Jewish and Latin-American cultural identities through the unique lens of poetry. This bilingual anthology enables readers to become *comadres* with a distinguished group of Latina poets who delve into a shared legacy of the Holocaust and exile as well as into a redefinition of belonging. Because Latinas have been oppressed for so long it is important to enlighten others by documenting what we've been through and allowing our personal histories to come alive through the richness of story and poetry. We give our struggles, dreams, experiences, and ideas new meaning when we collect them as a group and show them to the world.

As Latinas we are the ones responsible for transmitting culture to our families and children; *Telling to Live* and *Miriam's Daughters* perform a similar function by telling the stories of Latinas' lives to the outside world. By offering the gift of their testimony and poetry, the women who contributed to these books become *comadres* not only with their fellow contributors but with their thousands of readers, thus enlarging the circle to which we all belong.

Isabel Allende and the Power of *Comadre* Circles

Born in Peru in 1942, Isabel Allende moved to Chile at the age of three. In 1975, she was forced to flee the country with her husband and two children after a military coup ousted and killed her uncle, Chilean president Salvador Allende. She lived in Caracas, Venezuela for the next thirteen years and later immigrated to the United States, where she now lives. Isabel is the author of *The House of the Spirits; Paula; Aphrodite, Daughter of Fortune; Portrait in Sepia,* and a number of other books. Her works have been translated into more than twenty-seven languages. She also has written children's books, plays, and newspaper and magazine articles. She was editor of a feminist women's magazine in Chile; has been a journalist for television and film documentaries; has lectured throughout America and Europe; and has taught literature at the University of Virginia, Montclair College in New Jersey, and the University of California, Berkeley. While she has said that "the most significant awards that I have are the moving letters that my readers have sent me," she has received numerous literary awards from around the world, including Best Novel of the Year (Chile, 1983); Book of the Year (Germany, 1984); Premio Literario Colima Award (Mexico, 1986); XLI Bancarella Literary Award (Italy, 1993); Critics Choice Award (United States, 1996); Sara Lee Foundation Award (United States, 1998); and the WILLA Literary Award 2000 (United States, 2000).

As we began our conversation about the significance of *comadres*, Isabel told me about her need, early in her life, for *comadre* connections. Had it not been for her women friends, she might not have been able to reach beyond the limited choices afforded to females in the traditional Chilean culture into which she was born. "I have been a feminist since I was a baby," she said. "At a very early age I was furious because I realized that my mother had been a victim of society, of the church, of the patriarchal culture. My father abandoned her, so without money and without an education she had to be supported by her father and her brother. As any other person who depends on somebody else, she didn't have any rights. But I saw that the men in her family had all the freedom and liberties and rights that my mother didn't have."

Isabel was raised in a very traditional family, very Catholic and conservative: "My destiny was to be like my mother—to be only the wife of somebody and the mother of somebody. I didn't want to be like my mother, but I was born into a society where nothing else was possible." However, between the ages of twenty-five and thirty, in the 1960s, Isabel got together with six or seven other women in Chile, and their mission was to emulate the consciousness-raising that women in the United States and England were bringing about. In Chile such feminist consciousness was a novelty: "We started learning about the women's movement, and we went out into the streets, and to magazines, and to TV, and we started communicating these ideas to other women, about what women were doing elsewhere in the world. And Chilean women began to say to themselves, 'Hey, I never realized I am the servant of my husband!' Our rage was then transformed into action."

Today, of course, Isabel is the servant of no one. She practices her literary art to the benefit and delight of millions of readers and credits her women friends with helping her survive the traumas and up-heavals that she, like so many of us, has had to get through. She talked to me about how important the company of other women has been to her throughout her life: "You need the company of women in order to survive. Survive things like pregnancies, sickness, death. It's a visceral need, very *terrestre*. In my case, I have always been surrounded by other women. I came from a big family, and in addition to being raised by my mother, I also had many other *madres postizas*. And also friends who were my surrogate sisters. So I had an extensive family that I cre-ated myself. I was able to rely on them, and because of them I was able to keep forging ahead, even during the worst of times, times of much grief and sadness."

For the last ten years Isabel Allende has been getting together weekly with a group of six women. The honest, intimate sharing of ideas and emotions, and the uncritical acceptance with which the women listen to one another, have created an indestructible bond among them. "The thing is to create relationships with the women in this circle," Isabel says, "which is the fundamental aspect of democ-racy. In a circle, when nobody directs the group, nobody gives coun-seling or advice, where every single person is a witness to what is happening in the life of each other, we are all witnesses who listen care-fully and with compassion. And that's what creates change. Just by being together you can create a spiritual energy, very humane, that al-lows you to overcome situations like death in the family, infidelity, bankruptcy, cancer—all these problems that in the course of life we may have. With the support of this six-person group you can get through such life situations."

The philosophy on which Isabel's circle of women is based is found in the book *The Millionth Circle: How to Change Ourselves and the World* by Jungian analyst Dr. Jean Shinoda Bolen, one of the women in Isabel's group. Dr. Bolen talks about the need for women's wisdom and compassion to permeate our patriarchal society and how this can happen one "circle" at a time. Such circles of women sharing in the way that Isabel describes can engender more and more circles, until the "millionth" circle tips the scale and changes the world in a most profound way. It isn't as idealistic as it might sound, as Bolen reveals that this idea is based on the Morphic Resonance Hypothesis of biologist Rupert Sheldrake. A simplified version of Sheldrake's theory is embodied in the allegorical tale "The Hundredth Monkey," in which a group of island monkeys learn to wash their food before eating it and somehow pass this newly learned behavior on to monkeys with whom they never interact. One monkey first discovers that washing her food improves its taste, then teaches a few more monkeys, who in turn show others. The miraculous part of the theory is that once all the monkeys on the island are "schooled" in washing their food, the monkeys on a different island—with no direct contact to the original group of monkeys—also begin to wash their food. Essentially, the theory is that once a critical number of animals learn a particular behavior, that behavior automatically becomes part of what other similar groups of animals do.

Whether Sheldrake's theory is true or not, Jean Bolen believes, as does Isabel Allende and many, many others, that if women come together in small circles to practice compassion and nurturance, and other such circles are in turn created, then eventually a more life-affirming, supportive way of relating will permeate our society at large, and a more humane world will result. "We need a significant number of individuals to be open to creating a new spiritual, ecological, planetary change," Isabel says. "And to realize that humanity is just one family. If this happens, we can eliminate all our boundaries and the conflicts between races. Wars and other violence can be replaced by new means of dialogue. If we create enough circles, we will be able to do this."

The notion of forming a circle of women, which then becomes one of a million circles of nurturing women, fits in perfectly with our commitment to use our *comadre* connections to improve our lives and the well-being of our communities. When we commit to receiving and giving our female wisdom and compassion, we contribute not only to our personal growth and the expansion of Latina Power, but to the welfare of women and men throughout the world, who will benefit from our examples and our good works. When we work together with our *comadres*, our power increases, our strength is amplified, and there is no stopping us, whether our agenda is dealing with AIDS, domestic violence, depression, or Latina empowerment.

Isabel Allende continues to draw strength from the circle of women to whom she is committed. "Even if I am traveling and cannot go to the group," she says, "I know that the group is there for me. I remember them, think about them, and feel their energy. Because they are with me and I am with them. And this is what gives me strength, an extraordinary and concrete strength."

The kind of inner strength to which Isabel refers can accompany you throughout your life when you carry within you the wisdom and support of *comadres* who are always there for you.

How to Create a *Comadre* Circle

Whether your current goal is to move to another city, start a family, earn a college degree, leave your dead-end job to find a more fulfilling one, open your own business, or simply gather the self-confidence to pursue an as yet undefined goal, surrounding yourself with supportive *comadres* can provide the spiritual and emotional backing you need to get where you want to go. When *comadres* come together in a group to share their energy, wisdom, understanding, and spirituality each member becomes more than she was before. She is empowered not only by what the others have told her, but also by being listened to with dedication and compassion.

I invite you to form your own circle of *comadres* and to thereby join "the million circles." Whether your *comadre* circle is created for the purpose of working on career-related issues or a political agenda, as a healing support group or a general consciousness-raising group, the following guidelines will help you get started.

1. *Determine the purpose of your* comadre *circle.*

    Is it to lend emotional support to each other in the pursuit of your life goals? To share practical information that can be used in your careers? To accomplish a particular political objective? To help each other heal from traumatic or troubling life events such as domestic abuse, divorce, or illness? Support groups for battered women have helped bring about tremendously beneficial personal and societal changes, and studies have shown that cancer patients who participate in support groups live almost twice as long as those who don't. Perhaps the purpose of your circle is a more general one: to support each other in whatever is happening in your lives, whether it is related to career, parenting, politics, or a personal issue.

2. *Choose whom you want to be in your* comadre *circle.*

    Choose *comadres* who are trustworthy, emotionally stable, and committed to the purpose of the group. Make sure that those you invite to join your circle are willing to share as much time, interest, and energy as you are. An appropriate number of women is between five and fifteen. Smaller groups are preferable if you want the circle to be more intimate or more spiritual, while larger groups are more appropriate for business-related or networking purposes.

3. *At your initial meeting, establish logistics.*

    Decide where you will meet (including whether the meeting place will vary or stay the same), when, and how often. Also, decide whether or not food will be part of the gathering, and if so, who will provide it and when it will be served. Discuss as well whether you would like to have each *comadre* circle meeting focus on a particular issue or whether you want the freedom to bring up whatever topic arises, depending on the needs and circumstances of the members.

4. *At the first meeting, have each* comadre *tell the group how she hopes to benefit from the gathering.*

   If circle members are unknown to one another, also have everyone identify who they are, what they do, and any other pertinent information, depending on the purpose of the group.

5. *Make it clear at the outset that when one member of the group talks, everyone else listens.*

   Every member needs to be respected when she talks, and no secondary conversations should be taking place. You might want to adopt this practice used in Indian cultures: a "talking stick" is kept in the middle of the circle, and the person whose turn it is to speak takes the stick until she is finished, at which time she returns the stick to the center. No one may speak unless she holds the stick.

6. *Agree that you will each avoid "monologues," where one person uses up all the time talking and leaves no time for others to share.*

   This shows disrespect for the other *comadres* in the circle, and after a while members of the group will tune you out.

7. *Make sure everyone understands that the principle of equality governs the* comadre *circle.*

   Every woman is equal in importance; none is elevated above the rest. This sense of mutual, respectful, democratic sharing—along with the openness and trustworthiness displayed by every *comadre*—will contribute to the energy, wisdom, and spirituality of the circle.

8. *If yours is a spiritually oriented* comadre *circle, you might want to begin each gathering with a collective silence.*

   Every member detaches from the day's events and personal problems, meditates for a few minutes, and then comes back more centered and able to share. You may want to light some candles, play a piece of soothing music, or create a simple altar in the center of the circle, which could include an object that is particularly significant to the circle members or to the topic being discussed. An inspirational reading might also follow your collective silence.

9. *If you are forming a career-oriented circle, invite members to say what they expect from the group, what they wish to offer, and how they might help each other with their business or career.*

Some women may choose to provide services to each other, to trade services with each other, or to share potential business contacts with one another. It's important that everyone in the group is honest about what they want and not be ashamed to say that they expect to enhance their business or career in some way by being a member of the group. On the other hand, if you don't achieve the results you hope for right away, it's important to stay committed to the group anyway. Sooner or later the help you provide to others via your *comadre* connections will come back to you. Every career is related somehow to connecting with the appropriate people, and in your group of eight or ten or fifteen people someone will know someone else who will be able to connect you with what you need. Also remember that once you get what you want from the group, this is not a reason to abandon it—and then to return only when you need something else. This is going to be a circle of women in which you are all committed to sticking together and helping each other. You might all be in the same career field or not. But even if one of you is a stockbroker, another is a teacher, and another is a lawyer or a psychologist, each one can provide a different perspective on how to enhance your career, how to resolve conflicts, what works, and what doesn't. Every woman can provide something valuable if there is unity in the group and honesty among its members. The goal is for you to provide to others, and in turn that support will come back to you in a positive way—as an unexpected gift to you from the group.

10. *Reach out to women outside the Latina community.*

While some *comadre* circles might focus on issues solely related to Latinas, we don't necessarily have to confine ourselves to being *comadres* within our own culture. There is always a richness in getting to know women from other cultures, learning from them, and exchanging experiences and ideas. Reaching out in this way expands our lives—as well as the idea behind the connectedness of a million circles of women. We can have a commitment and a loyalty to our own and at the same time connect with all of society.

11. *Learn to be a good listener.*

In a *comadre* circle, as in any *comadre* relationship, being an attentive and uncritical listener is essential in order to ensure that the connection to your *comadre* is a supportive one. When you make yourself vulnerable by sharing your uncertainty about your career or by revealing something intimate in your life, you don't want to be criticized; you want to be heard. You don't want to be interrupted, and you don't need someone's opinion. You just want to express yourself and be heard by a compassionate and active listener. When we share with our *comadres* we usually just want our feelings to be acknowledged and validated. We're not seeking solutions. In fact, we may find our answers inside of ourselves in the simple process of being heard.

As the listener, you don't need to agree or disagree. Your role is not to come up with a new idea or advice, unless it is solicited. You are there to make this woman feel you are her *comadre,* that she is being nurtured by someone who respects her feelings, gives her the time and attention she needs, and understands what she is expressing. This orientation implies the complete absence of an authoritative or paternalistic attitude.

12. *Express your feelings honestly, without being judgmental.*

Being a good listener and not offering agreement or disagreement doesn't mean you should be untruthful. Once we know that our *comadre* is not truthful with us we cannot trust that person. And trust is crucial. If everybody can express their feelings honestly, then there is a better connection. How to do this without pushing your opinion onto someone else? Avoid comments that begin with "You should." Instead, articulate your own feelings with *"I feel that . . ."* statements. For example, "Hearing what you say about how harshly your boss treats you, *I feel that* if someone had treated me that way, I would . . ." This way you're talking about your own feelings and avoiding judgment of the other person.

If you're interested in reading more about women's circles in general, you might want to read *Sacred Circles: A Guide to Creating Your Own Women's Spiritual Group* by Robin Deen Carnes & Sally Craig.

Comadres as Mentors

A mentor can be a special type of *comadre*, because mentoring is like an aspect of mothering. It involves nurturing someone who has less experience, knowledge, or wisdom than you so that they can realize their life plans. Passing on the lessons we've learned throughout a lifetime is both personally gratifying and spiritually fulfilling, and being on the receiving end of such wisdom inspires us not only to take advantage of those lessons, but to share our own insights when it comes our turn to mentor.

While it is not uncommon for women to have male mentors, when the mentoring relationship is with a *comadre* the connection can be especially rich and beneficial. And the importance of someone who guides you and shows you the ropes in your chosen field cannot be underestimated. Successful Latinas in every field—from politics, business, and the professions to sports, science, and the arts—often talk about the crucial role their mentors played in helping them to believe in themselves and strive for their envisioned goals.

The word mentor derives from ancient Greece, from Homer's epic poem, *The Odyssey*. In the poem, Mentor is the most trusted friend and adviser of Odysseus, as well as the guardian and teacher of Odysseus's son, Telemachus. Adviser, friend, guardian, teacher—we embody each of those roles when we share our experiences in order to provide guidance to another person. A nurturing *comadre* mentor is one who encourages her "mentee" to develop her interests and strengths, and to pursue those objectives about which she feels most idealistic and passionate. She advises her mentee about the concrete steps she'll need to take to make her personal vision a reality. She helps her to recognize career-enhancing opportunities and challenges her to pursue them. And perhaps most important, a mentor *sincera* talks honestly with her mentee about her own experiences and the path that led to her success—including the inevitable setbacks along the way.

It's usually very common in women over fifty to want to mentor younger people. In midlife we are not as competitive as before, not as threatened by another's success, so we can feel proud of a younger woman, for example, whom we help to come up in the world. We each can give birth in different ways, and mentoring can be likened to a physical birth in that you're helping to launch another person's life. So by mentoring—by giving your experience, your insight, your discoveries about the way the world works—you are giving life, your life, to another woman. And she then integrates your life into her own. What gift could be more valuable? There is a vitality and an energy in the *comadre* mentor relationship because the exchange between the two of you is so mutually beneficial. One receives fulfillment from giving her wisdom, while the other gratefully uses that gift to pursue a fulfilling life.

It is in our nature to reach out to those who need help and to show them the way. Mentoring is a way for Latinas to empower each other by helping those with less experience to prepare for their chosen path, to avoid tripping over obstacles strewn along the way, and to build the confidence that comes with doing well what you love to do.

María Hinojosa's Mentors

CNN correspondent, anchor of NPR's *Latino USA*, and honored by *Hispanic Business* magazine as one of the one hundred most influential Latinos in the United States, María Hinojosa proudly asserts that her first mentor was her mom. She demonstrated to María that not only was it possible to both work outside the home and raise a family, it was also a joy. "My mom was a great example," María told me. "Every time that she was told no, she would go ahead and do it anyway. When she stopped being a full-time housewife and went to work in the hospital, she was firm in her decision. She wanted to have a career as well as a family. So she was the one who became my role model."

Maybe it doesn't sound like such a big deal to some women today, that working outside the home would represent such a victory. But the

women in María's mother's family, like so many Latinas of their generation, were obliged to go along with their husbands' demands to be
stay-at-home moms and housewives. Consequently, although María
talks about how strong and competent they are, her aunts never completed a professional career, having given it up to raise a family. "That
was the big difference between them and me," María says. "I was very
progressive, and I wasn't going to keep playing that game—leaving a
career to be solely a wife and mom. I had a Mexican reality very present, but my U.S. family—and the women that my mom knew—
showed me the other side. I understood my mother's dreams, and she
was very proud that she pushed her children to live life fully. It didn't
cross my mind that I would leave all of that for a man. My mom was an
inspiration. She loves her family, and that comes first, but she had a
voice, and she wanted to use it. So she fought for that."

Born in Mexico City, María moved to Chicago with her family
when she was only one-and-a-half years old. At the age of eighteen she
moved to New York to go to college. Coming from a family that encouraged girls to pursue higher education, going to college always had
been part of her plan, as it had been for her female cousins in Mexico.
While attending the prestigious Barnard College, however, María was
uncertain about her future ambitions. Trying to realistically identify
possible career options, she initially thought about working for the
United Nations or going into anthropology. She also dreamed about
being an actress in the theater. But when she became involved in radio
at Barnard it sparked her interest, and her dreams switched from theater to journalism. She wanted to be a television reporter, but at that
time had no role models: "There were no other Latinas doing TV reporting. It was like throwing yourself into the depths of the water."

María told me that there have been many people who inspired and
encouraged her as she made her way up the rungs of the journalistic
ladder. There are two friends in particular, however, whom she considers mentors. One is a woman named Sandy, a vice president at National Public Radio. Among many other things, Sandy taught María

the importance of acknowledging your own inexperience and seeking support from someone with more knowledge in your field—someone who just might know how to handle those moody bosses we've all come up against. "You have to be humble enough to reach out when you need help and direction," María says. "When I was younger I thought that I had to know it all, and do it all on my own, but Sandy's input has been very important to me at different moments in my career. As an executive of a network she has a great deal of experience. And one of the things she taught me is how to confront bosses when there is a certain type of conflict. She told me, before talking to a moody boss, you need to put a drop of 'honey' in your mouth."

While going it alone might sound heroic, without the benefit of a wise mentor guiding you along the path to your envisioned goal you could miss the opportunities to get there safely—or at all. The other mentor in María's life is someone she refers to as her "overall life coach." Interestingly, one of the first lessons she learned from this astute *comadre* named Andaye was that you don't have to be perfect to be someone's guide. "Andaye has had some very difficult times in her own life, and I know that she's not perfect," María says. "But that's how I learned that people don't need to be perfect, as I once thought they did. So I took her down from the pedestal I had put her up on. But she has always given me wise advice. Years ago I told her about a dream I'd had where I was flying and then fell down. It was a reflection of my fears at the time."

Andaye asked María, "What would happen if you let yourself fall down—in the dream or in real life?" and María answered, "I don't know." And then Andaye told her, "Well, the worst thing that can happen is that you would fall to the floor. And so what? Then you would get up." It was a very simple answer, but it made María open her eyes to the fears that had been controlling her life. "Andaye pointed out that your fears don't disappear after you're thirty or forty," María told me. "They only change. And learning how to manage them, you become stronger."

María's dream is very interesting because sometimes we are so concerned about falling down—not succeeding at something we want to attempt—that we paralyze ourselves. In every life there is some failure, but it doesn't have to mean breaking down—or crashing. It can mean that you fall in order to start again, not from scratch, but from a place of enhanced experience that will make it easier to navigate the course ahead. And with the help of a *comadre*, who shares her wisdom and gives you a better map for where you're headed, that course becomes more navigable still. Her guidance won't guarantee that you'll never fall, or even that you'll never sense that fear of falling, but your drop will be cushioned by her wise advice. So the bottom line is to reach out for help; there is a *comadre* mentor out there for you who has already fallen and figured out how to fly again.

Depending Too Much or Too Little on Your *Comadre* Connections

When it comes to developing our *comadre* connections, we want to make sure that we neither depend too much nor too little on our *comadres*. The following are some guidelines that will help you determine if you're slipping too far in one direction or the other.

If you sense that you're losing touch with your own goals, values, or beliefs in favor of someone else's, or if you find yourself asking a *comadre* to make decisions for you, you are probably relying too heavily on the advice of your *comadres*. Perhaps you are insecure about following through with your own objectives and need to feel aligned with a particular individual or group; however, when that need overshadows your own goals and ideals, that's when you run the risk of acting against yourself. We cannot rely on somebody else to chart the course for our life's journey, even if we trust their experience and wisdom. It is one thing to accept the support of our *comadre* as we're heading down a new path; it's something else to expect her to tell us what to do or to resolve our problems. In order to avoid leaning too hard on our *comadres*, we need to keep reminding ourselves that we each are responsible for our own decisions. Insecurity and mistakes are to be expected, but we can learn to handle the consequences of acting on our own behalf. Sharing ideas and experiences with your *comadres* doesn't mean that any one of them should take on the role of directing your life. You are the director.

On the other hand, when you don't take advantage of your *comadre* connections, because you feel you either should or can do it yourself, you isolate yourself unnecessarily. Whatever your desired goal, it becomes many times more difficult when you insist on pursuing it entirely by yourself. Often those who disconnect from others in this way end up feeling inadequate or abnormal, when in fact there are many women like them going through the same thing. And with each other's support the struggle becomes less of an uphill battle.

An important example of what can happen when women break out of that isolation and seek the support of those who are going through or have been through a similarly difficult experience is that of the survivors of domestic violence. One out of every three women is a survivor of domestic abuse, and while it is tough to break the cycle of violence by yourself, a support group can give you the emotional backup and practical advice to help you do it. Similarly, if you are struggling to find financial aid for a higher education, to break into a career whose doors seem closed to you, to take the entrepreneurial plunge, or even to deepen your spiritual awareness, never forget to reach out to your *comadres* for their help. Those who have been there and are willing to share their experiences with you can make the difference between lagging behind and leaping forward.

Another aspect of not being enough of a *comadre* is when we become competitive in a negative way. Being competitive is a positive thing when you recognize another person's achievements and use her example as inspiration. But when you're not confident enough in your own ability to grow and improve, you might be tempted to minimize or criticize what another person is doing in order to look better yourself.

This type of behavior is not in the *comadre* spirit, and it also won't help you to enhance your own abilities.

Together *Podemos*

As Latinas, we are well schooled in being there for each other no matter what, because we are accustomed to taking on the role of *comadre* in our families and communities. Now we are learning how to expand our *comadre* networks so that we can accomplish those things that will make our lives more fulfilling and complete. Throughout this chapter we've been hearing about the small miracles *comadres* can perform, from providing an understanding ear in the context of a supportive *comadre* circle to giving seasoned advice about handling one's boss with a honeyed phrase.

Another important example of our Latina connectedness is found in the groups of dedicated women protesting the horrors of political oppression. When we think about the most profound issues around which *comadre* circles have been organized, those in Latin America definitely come to mind. Courageous women have banded together to protest the murderous injustice of *los Desaparecidos*, people taken from their homes as punishment for their political views or those of their family.

For example, in Argentina, the *Madres de Plaza de Mayo* and the *Abuelas de Plaza de Mayo* used their anguish and outrage to organize against a government regime that engaged in the brutal violation of the most fundamental human rights. These women's children and grandchildren were among the thirty thousand persons who "disappeared" because they were suspected of antigovernment ideas. The *madres' y abuelas'* first action was to march arm-in-arm, day after day, in the center of the Plaza de Mayo in Buenos Aires. When the police demanded that one of the leaders show them her papers, she obliged by giving them the papers of all three hundred women in attendance. "It was a very important action for us," one participant recalled, "pointing out how unified we had become. It was all of us or none of us." These groups of mothers and grandmothers have worked on four levels: denunciations before national and foreign governments; appeals to the judiciary; advertisements in the press; and personal investigations. After years of searching, they have been able to locate many disappeared children and to provide victimized families involved in this struggle with lawyers, doctors, and psychologists.

Comadres have banded together as well in Chile, El Salvador, and Guatemala to protest the brutality of military regimes in those countries. As author Sonia Saldivar-Hull says in her book *Feminism on the Border,* these brave women, and those in Argentina, "transform the meaning and the political significance of 'mother.' "

Joining together to meet the needs of families during economic crises, women in Peru, Chile, and Argentina have formed *comedores populares,* purchasing food and cooking meals for groups of fifteen to fifty households and providing yet another example of *comadres* pooling their human resources in times of need.

Comadre networking can advance such life-and-death causes as trying to free the victims of political violence as it also can enrich the lives of those of us fortunate enough to live in a more stable and peaceful political environment. When we join together as *comadres* to further the causes of justice, peace, freedom, and women's empowerment, our voices cannot be ignored. As Margaret Mead put it, "Never doubt that a small group of committed citizens can change the world; indeed, it is the only thing that ever has."

The *Diplomática's* Discretion

I learned about being a diplomat from being raised in a large family
of seven children. One day your brother could be your worst enemy,
but the next day you're teaming up with him against somebody else.
Also, in my family, as in most Latino families, it's assumed that your
elders know more than you do, so you defer to them and you listen to
what they have to say. You learn when to talk, with whom to talk,
what subjects are okay to discuss, and what to avoid discussing. In
my family I learned what is worth fighting for and what is not, and
not to make waves every single time. I was also taught not to speak
out in a negative or unacceptable way.

And you know what? This kind of formality and courtesy—this
particular way of being diplomatic—is very important in politics. As
a congresswoman, the most important thing I've discovered about
being diplomatic is that when you're patient and really listen to the
other person, you can learn a lot about their point of view. And that
knowledge can help you accomplish your own goals.
— Representative Loretta Sánchez,
U.S. Congress

Listening respectfully to those whose opinions we might not share,
avoiding hot-button topics when the timing isn't right, being courteous
to family and strangers alike—these comprise a code of conduct so
intrinsic to most Latinas that it may hardly seem worthy of mention.
And yet we all know how stressful and contentious life can become
when we don't practice our natural ability to be *diplomáticas*. Learning from our female relatives how to mediate between members of
our large extended families is part of every Latina's experience. In

our culture women are expected to not only keep the peace among those who share a household but to bridge the gaps between dissonant family factions, bringing everyone together so that the larger circle of *la familia* is preserved. We probably take these negotiating and peacekeeping skills for granted, but they are closely related to the abilities that seasoned politicians and career diplomats have had to cultivate.

Diplomacy is a crucial element not only in politics and international relations but also in every field of endeavor in which humans must get along with each other. Without it, corporate decisions couldn't be arrived at, schoolchildren couldn't be reasoned with, doctors couldn't relate to their patients, and softball players couldn't count on their teammates. In this chapter we're going to find out how accomplished Latinas have inherited this valuable aptitude in their families of origin and then used it to become the successful women they are. Knowing how to be tactful, how to use discretion, and how to communicate effectively with coworkers, clients, and bosses can mean the difference between losing the trust of those with whom you work and forging strong career relationships that ensure your success. The women who share their stories in this chapter will reveal just how *diplomacia* has benefited the work they are so passionately involved in.

From Outsider to Insider
TV Producer María Pérez-Brown

Creator and executive producer of *Taina,* the top-rated live-action series on Nickelodeon about a fifteen-year-old girl who balances the world of her traditional Puerto Rican family with the modern world of her school and friends, María Pérez-Brown made an important discovery about *diplomacia* early in her life. As she told me about the amazing path that took her from Puerto Rico to Brooklyn to Yale, and then from NYU law school to a creative career in television, it became clear that for María being a diplomat began with learning how to play by the rules.

Born in Puerto Rico to a poor family, María's grandparents worked in the sugar cane fields, and her mother had to start working as a young girl in order to help the family survive. Married at fourteen, María's mom had her first child at fifteen, the second one at sixteen, and by eighteen she was the mother of four. María is the second child. "It was a very hard life for my mother," María told me. "She had to fight hard just to keep us all alive. We always had something to eat, but for days we may have had only white rice. My parents were separated, and my mom decided she wasn't going to raise her children in Puerto Rico, with all its poverty, because she didn't want any of us to repeat her own story. She wanted to change our lives. So she moved to New York and got a job sewing in a factory, while my *abuelos* and *tíos* took care of us kids back home. And in less than a year she came back and got us. I was six years old."

One of the first things María figured out when she entered elementary school in Brooklyn was the importance of rules. It turns out that this lesson—intrinsic to becoming a savvy *diplomática*—would serve her well as she continued with her education and eventually entered the career she now enjoys. But it all started in the second grade. "At six years old, I was totally an outsider," she said. "In Brooklyn, without any English, going into second grade, I had to learn to communicate with my teacher. I had to learn a new language and also translate for my mom. All of my environments were totally new, so I had to figure out what the rules were, how things were done. And I had to work within those rules somehow."

When María reached seventh grade, the family moved to Connecticut. She continued to do well in school, and in high school received four university scholarships. Again, the significance of rules and of being a *diplomática* played a part in her adjustment to new challenges: "At my elementary school in Brooklyn, at my junior high and high schools in Connecticut, and then at Yale and at NYU law school—in each of those instances I had to learn from scratch, from zero. I continued to figure out the rules in each case, and how to diplomatically work within those rules so I could learn what I needed to do to succeed. I didn't have any idea what the university was about, and the first thing I discovered was that people were very driven and ambitious."

After receiving her law degree from NYU, where she had loved studying international law, especially history and politics and everything that related to the culture of Latin America, María landed her first job. But it was in tax law, and she was bored with the work. She realized she was neglecting her interest in entertainment and writing. So she considered how she might combine her interests. She started doing pro bono legal work for writers and producers who couldn't afford an attorney. Helping them with contracts and representing them on various projects, such as turning a book into a movie, María learned a lot about the film and TV business. She eventually had so many clients that she decided to start her own business. "My kitchen table became my new law office," she now recalls.

Knowing little about production but accomplished in writing, as well as the business end of the TV and film industries, María wrote her first script. It was for *Gullah Gullah Island*, a children's program about a big yellow frog and his family who live on an island off the south coast of the United States. María became associated with a producer, and together they sold the idea to Nickelodeon. In the first season they had twenty episodes. The show ran for four years, and currently eighty-five episodes are being shown on Noggin (a digital cable station). After the success of *Gullah Gullah Island* Nickelodeon asked for new ideas, and María developed the program *Taina*, which was named Best Children's Series for 2002 by the Imagen Foundation and the American Latino Media Arts Awards.

And how does she use her *diplomacia* skills at this stage in her career? Having adjusted successfully to "foreign" environments throughout her life—to the foreign country where she didn't know the language, the college campus where academic culture was unfamiliar to her, and the entertainment business which is still largely unfamiliar with Latinos—María has realized that learning the rules is key to becoming an insider. It's only by familiarizing yourself with how things work and what is acceptable that you can strategize how to fulfill your vision diplomatically. When I asked her how a successful Latina in one of the world's most competitive fields works within—and then manages to bend—the rules, María gave me more specifics:

"At Yale I found support from upper classmates, who showed me the way. They taught me the rules, how I had to behave, and then it was up to me to change the rules in a way that would be convincing or acceptable to those in power. Today I'm the only Latina in this [working] environment. When I go to meetings, there are sometimes two or three Latinos, but I am the only Latina. You need to be a diplomat in any circle, especially when you are the outsider. If someone offends me, I've learned that it's up to me to respond diplomatically. If I respond simply by saying 'You're a racist' that's not always the right thing to do, because then I may be perceived as a big complainer. If you're a producer being considered for a particular show, and you're perceived as antagonistic, you won't be given the opportunity to work. So I've learned how to make compromises without compromising my integrity and values. I've learned to play by the rules, to get inside—and then make changes from the inside. You see what the circumstances are and what the right timing will be to make a particular political stand. And, in fact, just being a Latina in this environment is already a political stand."

Having learned to use her *diplomacia* to become a dynamic, creative force in a business she loves, María now feels there is no place in the world she can't go. "It's just that I have to learn the rules first," she says. "Once you learn how to survive in a particular environment, even if it's strange or different, there's nothing that you can't do."

Finding Common Ground with Your Opponent
Social Activist Dr. Antonia Pantoja

Perhaps the most important element of *diplomacia* is knowing how to deal with those who challenge you or with whom you disagree. Whether it's a matter of getting along with your husband or reaching an agreement that satisfies both your position and that of a hostile client, knowing how to approach potential adversaries in a diplomatic way is an invaluable skill.

The late Dr. Antonia Pantoja—founder of the Puerto Rican Forum, the Latino Youth Organization ASPIRA, and the community organization in Puerto Rico PRODUCIR, an educator and activist who was involved in building stronger Puerto Rican and minority communities, and the recipient of the Presidential Medal of Honor under President Clinton—was a *diplomática* who had honed her people skills over the years to the point where she could negotiate brilliantly with those in power in order to advance the causes of workers and poor people.

Looking back at her early life in Puerto Rico, it might appear as if Antonia was a negotiator even at the age of six. It was then that she found a way to challenge her grandmother on the touchy subject of attending church. She told me about this and other life experiences as we discussed the issue of *diplomacia*. Sadly, our conversation was one of the last interviews, if not the last one, in her life. "I was raised by my grandparents, and my grandmother would send me to church every Sunday with a friend of mine from the neighborhood," Antonia recalled. "She would give me some money, an *ofrenda* to take to church for catechism. But instead of going to church, sometimes my girlfriend and I would go to the other side of the city to have an ice cream, to a place that still exists—called *La Bombonera*. One day the bishop started quizzing me and my friend to see if we knew our catechism well enough to have our first communion, and I wasn't able to answer the questions. So they told my *abuela* that I wasn't attending classes. And she reprimanded me, got very upset at me, and asked me why I wasn't going to church. That's when I tried to negotiate with her by pointing out what we had in common. 'Abuela,' I asked her, 'why do you want *me* to go when *you* don't go to church yourself?' "

Although her grandmother still insisted that Antonia finish her catechism classes, even at such a young age Antonia had grasped the notion of finding common ground. She didn't like going to church — and neither did her grandmother! And by pointing this out to her "adversary" she was practicing to be the diplomatic negotiator she would later become.

Antonia was also enlightened by the harrowing experiences of her grandfather, a *tabaquero* worker and labor organizer. Learning early on that one had to fight just to provide the bare essentials for your family, Antonia credited her *abuelo* with showing her the meaning of courage. When they were living in the slums of San Juan, her grandfather started an organization of tobacco workers, which had not existed previously in Puerto Rico: "The men would come to our house and discuss salaries, and my *abuelo* was a real leader. He attracted other people and they would follow him. They started to create a labor union, and at some point went on strike. They gathered in front of a restaurant, but they were assaulted with hot oil, by the owners. When my *abuelo* came home, his legs were burned, and that left me with a very powerful impression, because I saw how the poor people were treated when they were only asking for a better salary. I saw the abuse, and this would give me the courage later in life to be strong. If not, life eats you up. From then on, I started to become a person who would not accept things as they are."

Antonia had to lobby her grandparents to get permission to go to high school, since it had been assumed that she would forego such a privilege to help out in the fields. Antonia's uncle spoke up on her behalf, telling her grandmother that she wouldn't be good as a worker because she was too small. (Another lesson in *diplomacia:* One way of getting what you want in life is by pointing out to your adversary how they will benefit by what you are proposing — in this case, the benefit of

not having a worker who would be too small to do the work). The lob-
bying paid off, Antonia went to school, and eventually, after two years
of college at the Universidad de Puerto Rico, became an elementary
school teacher. Having read novels that romanticized life in the country, she asked to be assigned a teaching position in the countryside.
Traveling to work by pickup truck and horse, she taught in a small
Puerto Rican town for six months. Her experience there opened her
eyes to more than just the challenges of teaching. "The people in that
little town worked from sunup to sundown, and I was fascinated by
their way of life," Antonia told me. "It was a liberating experience for
me. They cooked only with fire and wood in the village, which meant
that everything tasted very smoky. So I didn't have an appetite much
of the time and often couldn't eat. I taught in a big room where I had
first, second, and third grade all together, so I had to create a way of
teaching the three groups at the same time—but I enjoyed it very
much. Although I was only eighteen at the time, even the parents of the
children would come to me for counseling, because I was the teacher
for the whole town and seen as an authority figure. It was in that village that I started to learn about people, how to relate to and teach people. I had to create a new scenario for myself."

Antonia created another new scenario for herself a short while
later when she and a friend—exasperated with the bureaucracy inherent in the educational system in Puerto Rico at the time—decided to
move to New York. Her new destination represented a glorious dream
for Antonia, but moving to the United States forced her to confront the
dark realities of racism and capitalist practices, as well as the fascinating diversity of a multiethnic country. She had read the poems of Pedro
Salinas, which created an image in her mind of her voyage to New
York as a path to her dream. "I dreamed about the Statue of Liberty,"
she told me, "which I had seen so many times in the movies and that my
mother had talked to me about, because she had been in New York
once. For me, going to New York was like a wonderful fairy tale."

But arriving in the States during World War II, Antonia came face to face with her first disillusionment: "We stopped first in New Orleans, and of course there was a lot of discrimination in the South then. Because I am black I became aware of it immediately. My girlfriend and I went to eat lunch with two young men from our high school whom we had met on the ship, and in the diner nobody came to take our order. So we had to buy our food in a market. Later, we went to the movies, and after we bought our tickets, the usher told us to go to the second floor, even though we wanted to sit on the first floor. When the movie ended, we noticed that only blacks were on the second floor—because only whites were allowed downstairs. Later, at the train station as we were boarding for New York, we heard the black porter calling out, 'Niggers to the back! Niggers to the back!' "

For three days on the train Antonia kept dreaming of the Statue of Liberty. Her dream had her coming into New York by sea, sailing by the lovely statue. "Instead, we arrived on this train into the stomach of the monster—the 34th Street station. . . . Still, I looked up at the dome of the station, and it had all the constellations—and I was in love with astronomy! We were like greenhorns, from top to bottom, with our little luggage bags tied together with string." Antonia and her friend took a taxi from the station to the apartment house in the Bronx where they were to stay with another friend. The elderly woman who answered the door there said, "Oh, you must be the Filipino girls. Your friend is waiting for you," unaware of the difference between Puerto Ricans and Filipinos. Once inside they noticed there was no electricity, only candles. The woman offered them showers and something to eat, and they were appreciative but wondered why the room was so dark. They later found out that the woman was Jewish, and it was *shabbat*, the sabbath, which was why they only had candles burning instead of electric lights. "That was my first contact with a Jewish family," Antonia recalled, "and that was when I started to learn about other cultures in New York."

After working in a radio factory and a children's lamp factory, Antonia was asked to be a designer at another lamp factory. She had been recognized as someone with talent and a university background, and her response to the offer was diplomatically forthright. "I said, 'Of course I will become the designer, if you pay me more.' " In her position as designer Antonia maintained relationships with the workers, most of whom were also Puerto Ricans. She found out that they needed clothing to wear to work, as well as a sofa in the rest room, in case someone felt sick. She went to the owner and asked him about these things, to which he replied that such benefits were not necessary. At this point Antonia had to test her ideals and her diplomatic skills — and she discovered that she was walking in her *abuelo*'s footsteps.

"I realized that the owner I worked for was very gentle and kind with respect to some things," Antonia said, "but not others. So I called a friend of mine who belonged to a union of electricians, and he came and helped me organize the workers to join his union." When Antonia went to talk to the owner, however, he became very upset. Having found out that she was the one who had started the union organizing effort, he asked her, "How can you do this when I have been like a father to you?" And she answered, "I don't need a father, thank you very much." It was then that Antonia realized that she was engaged in the same struggle as her *abuelo*—organizing to make things better for the workers. "I also realized that I had to continue taking on that role, even if the owner was upset at me."

In learning to negotiate with the owner of the lamp factory, Antonia managed to stick to her position while still keeping the lines of communication open and friendly. She told me that throughout her career in New York she learned a lot about the Jewish community, of which this owner was a part. Many had once been in the same position as the Puerto Rican workers who were now seeking to improve their conditions, and in fact had been instrumental in building the labor movement in New York. While the initial dialogue with the owner of the lamp factory represented a confrontation of differing positions, Antonia went on to talk about the common ground between the Jews and Puerto Ricans of New York City: "The Jews had once been on the bottom rung but were now moving up the ladder, and the Puerto Ricans had further to climb. But we could understand each other because the Jewish people didn't belong either. We shared the role of outsider in the eyes of mainstream Americans. We would disagree, but then discuss things and come to a compromise. As for me personally, I learned to relate to people who were different—because we needed each other. And I think it's important to see the whole picture, not just one reality, because we are all like a little screw in an enormous mechanical system, and you have to perceive the whole without losing sight of the fact that you are that little screw."

In that initial experience as a labor organizer Antonia was able to both maintain a good relationship with the factory owner and negotiate a decent contract for the workers. How did she manage to do that? When we realize that we have much more in common with other people than we might initially think, our world opens up and *diplomacia* comes more easily to us. When we are willing to learn from others—while at the same time remaining focused on what we want to achieve—we become *diplomáticas expertas*.

Antonia's legacy of programs in youth leadership, education, business development, and training in the Puerto Rican community are a testament to her unwavering yet diplomatic activism.

Listening with Openness:
Congresswoman Loretta Sánchez

There is an essential feature of our Latino upbringing that we probably don't realize contributes to our being good *diplomáticas*, and that is the respect we show to our elders. With all the emphasis in American society on the youth culture, it is nice to know that in *our* culture we pay close attention to the opinions and wisdom of the oldest members of our community. You wouldn't think that this custom would necessarily benefit a politician, but in my conversation with U.S. Representative Loretta Sánchez, she explained why this is the case. As her quote at the opening of this chapter revealed, when you learn as a child to defer to your elders, to listen courteously to them and honor what they have to say, you not only develop good listening skills but a sense of respect, both of which are needed in order to be an effective politician.

"The basic thing about diplomacy is the structure of being formal," Loretta told me. "The American way is different from many other cultures around the world. The emphasis here is on being an individual and thinking for yourself. And Americans learn to do that because our opinion is important, even when we're children. But in my family, and in most Latino families, it's assumed that your elders know more than you do, so you defer to them and you listen to what they have to say. You learn how to be a diplomat as a child because you defer to the adults for their opinion, you don't challenge them. You learn when to talk, with whom to talk, what subjects are okay to discuss, and what to avoid discussing. And there are certain topics you never discuss—in my family those were sex, money, and violence."

A subject that *was* discussed in Loretta's home as she was growing up was politics—and there was a diversity of opinion even within her immediate family. Perhaps it was listening intently to these lively discussions, and joining in as well, that set the stage for Loretta's future political career. "My father was a businessman, so he had more of a Republican mind, but my mother was a homemaker and had more compassion, so she was more of a Democrat," Loretta explained. "At the dinner table we always talked about politics, and my father had a pretty hard line. As a businessman he talked about why taxes should be cut. And then my mother would say, 'Yes, but we need money for educating children and for the mentally ill to stay in hospitals.' As for politicians, my father always told us, 'Never be a politician, because the good ones get shot, like Kennedy, and the bad ones are corrupt and bad.' So when I decided to run for political office, my father couldn't understand it. Now he sees the good things that I'm doing and he's always worrying about me."

It seems that Loretta inherited the sensibilities of both her parents.

Like her dad, she was initially business-oriented, and like her mom, she was always thinking about how to improve the lives of those in the community who needed help. The impetus to become involved in politics was her concern for the educational welfare of children. But prior to making that initial decision to run for office she relied on her mother's advice for the direction her life should take. "Before I got into politics I was an investment banker, and I had my own business," Loretta told me. "But I had some extra time, so I went to my mom and asked her for ideas about what I should do. She said, 'Why don't you do something to help children in school?' "

That's when Loretta started to work with a summer math and science enrichment program in Anaheim that helped prepare junior high school students for college. She noticed that only twenty children had signed up for the program, and she wanted to try to increase that number. So she talked to the school board and the mayor about trying to recruit students for the program, but was unable to get anywhere. Out of her frustration, and her anger over Proposition 187, a statewide referendum that proposed kicking undocumented children out of schools, Loretta decided to alter her career path dramatically. She committed to putting all her energies into the improvement of education and making a difference in her community and elsewhere by becoming a politician.

Today Loretta is a member of the U.S. House of Representatives Committee on Education and the Workforce, is working to improve educational opportunities for disadvantaged kids, and is at the forefront of all educational initiatives moving through Congress. She started a program called "Gear Up" in Santa Ana, California, in conjunction with various universities, which helps prepare middle-school students in math and science so that when they graduate from high school they will qualify for a scholarship to go to a university. The program is now in effect across the nation.

We all know that in order to get legislation through Congress in the United States one must convince those who might not initially agree with you to support your position, if not your vision. One important strategy is to listen with openness to the other side of the issue — so that you'll be able to make your case effectively. This is a diplomatic skill that all of us can use, whether we're trying to push forward an education bill in Congress, like Loretta Sánchez; win appropriate benefits for fellow workers, like Antonia Pantoja; reach an equitable agreement with a prospective client; or even guide a teenage daughter who is trying to convince us of the benefits of body piercing.

As a Latina, Loretta Sánchez had the training in *diplomacia* that continues to inform the way she relates to people, conducts business, and pursues the social programs she values. Having grown up in a Latino household, she knows when to refrain from speaking up, how to treat others with respect, and how to synthesize differing points of view to advance her goals. She maintains that listening is the key: "As a congresswoman, the greatest lesson I've learned about being diplomatic is to listen to the other person and be patient. Listening to what someone is telling you — with openness — you can really learn from that person. And really 'hear' what that person is telling you."

Becoming a Better Listener

As Loretta Sánchez's story made clear, being a good listener can be what distinguishes a savvy *diplomática* from a self-centered manipulator. Have you ever been at a party or business gathering and had the disconcerting experience of knowing the person you're talking with isn't really listening to a word you're saying? Maybe their eyes are darting around the room, checking to see who else has arrived; or perhaps they're looking at you but have that glazed-over look, revealing that their attention is definitely somewhere else. Making a concerted effort to be a careful and respectful listener is vital if you are to understand how your viewpoint differs from that of others — and how you might bridge the gap between you.

Here are some suggestions for enhancing your listening skills. I think you'll find that they can help you transform your conversations—whether with friends, family, or colleagues—from static monologues to dynamic dialogues from which both parties can learn more about the other.

1. Look into the eyes of the person you're talking with. This will help you maintain contact and avoid the impression that your attention is elsewhere.
2. Concentrate fully on what the person is saying rather than on what your response is going to be. The objective is to learn more about them.
3. Give the person time to articulate their thoughts. Don't interrupt or attempt to finish their sentences for them.
4. After you have listened carefully to the other person, very briefly summarize what they've just said, so that they know you understand what they're trying to communicate to you. For example: "What I'm hearing you say is that you'd like to have more creative responsibility at work."
5. After first acknowledging what the other person has said, you can give your opinion or input, if it has been solicited. But don't veer off onto a subject that's unrelated to what the other person was talking about. When we do this, we can be perceived as self-centered and poor listeners. For instance, if someone is telling you about a painful experience, sometimes the worst thing you can do is to say something like, "Oh, yes, it happened to me too and this is what I went through . . ." It's better to listen and to sympathize, rather than to provide unsolicited information.

Congressional Sister Power—and the Power Behind It
Congresswoman Linda Sánchez and Her Mother, María Macías

I did not anticipate when we began planning this book that I would be interviewing *two* U.S. Congresswomen from the Sánchez family. Making history as the first sisters to serve in the U.S. Congress, these two dedicated and dynamic Southern California Latinas are an inspiration to all of us. In talking with Linda Sánchez about *diplomacia*, like her sister Loretta, she brought up the benefits of being raised in a large

Latino family. She told me that having to get along with so many siblings with different points of view contributed to the development of skills that are essential to her work as a lawyer and congresswoman.

"In our family every person had their own perspective on things," Linda said. "So you had to learn to listen to everybody, process the information, and then try to build a consensus. Sometimes, when one of us kids got into trouble, we would get together and try to talk through how best to face our fairly strict, disciplinarian father. We would have these intense negotiating sessions before going to my dad and admitting whatever it was that we weren't supposed to have done."

Linda later put her negotiating skills to use as a lawyer working on behalf of the labor movement. Advocating for a just cause, being willing to compromise with the other side, and demonstrating an authentic spirit of cooperation are all part of a *diplomática*'s strategy, as Linda explained to me. "You have to work with parties that may be very far apart on what each side wants," she said. "Slowly you try to build consensus or a common ground where both can agree. And what I've found in negotiating to get two sides to come together is that you have to make people see that what they're giving up is less important than what they're gaining."

During the years that separated Linda's childhood negotiating sessions and her career as a labor movement negotiator, she took her inspiration from an amazingly energetic and determined woman: her mother, María Macías. Born in Mexico, María had worked as a secretary for the Banco Nacional de México in Mexicali before moving to the States. She married at nineteen and had seven children. Active in the PTA and fundraising at her children's school, she was also a Girl Scout leader, a Boys' Club organizer, and a sewing teacher. She instilled the desire for a college education in all of her sons and daughters, not only by *telling them* to get their college degree, but by *showing them* how it's done. After twenty years of being an involved, activist mom, María entered the university at age forty, at a time when it was not common for older students to do so. She earned both her college degree and a teaching credential. How did it feel for María at the time to begin an academic career?

"I had seven children at home and I had to study at night, so I often felt it was a mountain that I couldn't climb," María told me. "At times, I thought about leaving. But after sweating through each exam, I would come back the next day and continue on. I learned that I could get through even the toughest obstacles. My children saw me going through this, and it definitely had an impact." As for María's husband, he presented much resistance at first: "He didn't support me because — you know how Latinos are. They want the woman to be in front of the stove. So even when I left his food for him — and all he had to do was warm it up — that was not enough. But he didn't interfere with my going to the university. Because I told him, 'If you love me as I am, you will have to accept me as I am — and I'm going to school.' He's twelve years older than me, so if something were to happen to him, what would I do to support myself?"

Linda Sánchez remembers being in elementary school when her mom went back for her college degree — and how her commitment provided motivation to all the kids in the family: "She used to come home, and she'd have her homework, and she'd say, 'Hey, all of you need to do your homework now. Your mother's doing her homework too. We'll all do our homework together.' And so we would all sit at the dining room table doing our homework together. Mom was the example." And when she went on to get her teaching credential and was obliged to pass a teaching exam, María didn't pass it the first time. She was very disappointed, but also very determined. She studied harder than ever and passed it the second time. "Watching her struggle," Linda said, "I learned that you can't give up just because things don't happen for you the first time around."

Just as María inspired her children, they in turn helped her. She says her daughters helped her with her math and the essays she had to write, correcting her English here and there. (She helped them with their Spanish, insisting that they not lose their command of it.) When things didn't always happen according to her plan, María was the *aguantadora,* determined to make it no matter what. She told me she thinks about that funny little song about the *cucaracha* when she remembers how determined she was to complete her degree—even when it seemed that every time there was an exam one of her kids would get sick! "You have to keep going like the *cucaracha.* You know, *'La cucaracha, la cucaracha, ya no puede caminar, porque no tiene, porque le falta, las patitas de atrás.'* She can't walk anymore because she doesn't have any hind legs—but you have to do like the *cucaracha* who cannot walk but keeps going anyway."

Today María Macías is enjoying her career as a bilingual teacher, but she's not about to rest on her laurels. The woman from Mexicali who inspired her seven children to strive for the best they could be—including two who are the first sisters to serve in the U.S. Congress—told me enthusiastically about her future plans. "When you start school, you take one class and you want more and more. Now that I'm going to retire, I'm going to take two more classes that I need to complete my master's in education. And I'm also going to take some art classes. I'm not going to stay home—I'm going back to school!"

And Congresswoman Linda Sánchez continues to take her cue from her mom's passionate dedication to a fulfilling life. She is following her own passion, which is the struggle for social justice and equality. In the mostly male world of law, government, and politics, she owes her *diplomática*'s consensus-building savvy and her *aguantadora*'s passionate determination to María.

A Diplomatic Attitude
Olympic Gold Medal Softball Pitcher Lisa Fernández

Deemed one of the best softball players in history, a record-setting pitcher who pitched five consecutive perfect games during USA Softball's pre-Olympic tour (including a game in which she struck out all twenty-one batters!) and the winner of two Olympic gold medals (in

1996 and 2000), Lisa Fernández is a genuine star. But she is also a team player. And in our conversation about the importance of *diplomacia,* she told me that in order for any team to function as a cohesive unit each member has to incorporate a certain element of diplomacy into their communication with the others. With a degree in psychology and a position as assistant coach of the University of California, Los Angeles's Bruin softball team, Lisa speaks from experience and with authority.

"When you play a team sport, attitude is important," Lisa maintains. "For example, when you make an error, how are you going to deal with that? How is the team going to deal with that? If a teammate isn't doing something right, how do you communicate to her in order to bring up her level of play so that the team doesn't suffer? That's what you learn playing a team sport: how to sit down with that player and explain to her how important she is and how integral she is to the team, and how her actions affect the team in a positive and a negative way."

I think Lisa touches on something here that is an extremely valuable asset of the wise *diplomática:* the ability to be positive while giving constructive criticism. When you are faced with the unenviable task of having to tell someone they're not going about something in quite the right way—whether it's your teammate, colleague, employee, or child—it's so important to stress the positive along with the negative. None of us likes to be criticized, but if someone first points out our strengths, before confronting us with what we need to improve on, doesn't it then become easier for us to accept their criticism?

Lisa was very fortunate to have had supportive parents who helped her develop not only her physical talents but the interpersonal skills she needs as a coach and team member. Her father, a semipro baseball player from Cuba, and her mother, a Puerto Rican who grew up in New York playing stickball, raised Lisa to enjoy the challenges of sports. Unlike many other parents at that time, including Latinos, who felt that athletics were for boys only, Lisa's mom and dad encouraged her to be physically active and strong. "Ever since I was nine or ten years old, my dad was always so proud of how strong I was," she told me. "He would say, 'Show me how strong you are,' motioning me to show him the muscles in my arm. And when I made a muscle, he'd say, 'Good! You gotta be strong to hit the ball out of the infield!' " That validation was important to Lisa, because she and her parents knew that she was going to have a strong, athletic body and that she could develop the skills to go with it, and they were always supportive of her being as active as she wanted to be. "I never had to worry about body image or anything like that," she recalled gratefully.

Lisa also didn't have to worry that her father might agree with the insinuations of some of his friends, who kept asking him, after Lisa graduated from high school and then college, why his daughter was still playing softball. Why wasn't she getting married and having children, like so many other Latinas in their community? Lisa's father had his own way of demonstrating to his inquisitive friends why Lisa was following her own path: "What he did was, he took the bat and glove with my name on them—I have an endorsement contract so they're sold to kids in the stores—and then he took my Olympic medals, and showing those to his friends, he would say, 'This is why my daughter still plays softball!' With both my dad and my mom it was never about 'You shouldn't be doing that stuff 'cause that's not what ladies do.' "

Despite the fact that there were few female or Latina athletes as role models when Lisa was growing up ("Nancy López was really the only Hispanic woman that I heard about being successful in sports"), Lisa succeeded in becoming an accomplished athlete—and is now a role model herself. While she may not be able to practice *diplomacia* on the pitcher's mound, she is a model diplomat off the field, where positive communication with teammates and opponents is as important to the success of her game as is physical prowess. When I asked if she had ever been treated undiplomatically by another softball player, she told me about a particularly stinging incident—and how she used it to her advantage. "During the Olympics, we lost a game to the Australian team. A girl got a home run off me, and we lost the game two to one.

Three months later I got a postcard with a picture of the girl who hit the home run on the shoulders of her teammates, celebrating the victory. On the back it just said, 'See you in Japan.' I didn't take too kindly to that." Lisa told me that she hates to lose and would do anything to win, but "you never want to rub it in or put down your opponent, you know? But the postcard was motivation—to push me to be better. In fact, it inspired me. I'm continuing to compete at the age of thirty-four—and I'm planning on going to the Olympics in 2004!"

Lisa is a passionate believer in girls having the opportunity to participate in team sports, and she's pleased that more girls and young women have that opportunity today than when she was growing up. She feels strongly that sports help develop not only our physical abilities, but our confidence and life skills as well, including how to communicate diplomatically with fellow players. "Athletics is such an enjoyable way to learn about things, like how to succeed, how to deal with failure, how to be competitive, how to perform under pressure, and how to communicate. When you're on a team you have to be able to communicate with each other. You're not always going to get along, and knowing how to talk to your teammates when something's not going right—that's so important."

Each of us has to incorporate the spirit of teamwork into our daily lives in some form or other. And I think if we remember Lisa's attitude about being positive and approaching criticism of others in a diplomatic, constructive way, our efforts will more likely benefit the team as a whole and us as individuals.

Overly Diplomatic . . . or Not Diplomatic Enough

Striking the proper balance between being overly diplomatic and not diplomatic enough requires finesse and experience. Again, Latinas have usually witnessed or engaged in *diplomacia* within their large families, so for many of us it shouldn't be that difficult to practice it outside the home. Here are some guidelines for knowing when you're headed too far in one direction or the other.

When you are too *diplomática*, you end up sacrificing your position or opinion for the other person's. You may do this because you fear being rejected or seen as *la ridícula*, or perhaps there is the possibility you could actually lose your job if you stand up for yourself. If you're afraid to come out and say what you know to be fair or correct, think about exactly what is at stake. If it's a small enough issue so that you can let it go without losing your sense of integrity, that's fine. But watch out for the tendency to sweep your own position under the rug; no relationship, job, or career move is worth the loss of your essential values. Being diplomatic doesn't mean pleasing others more than you please yourself.

On the other hand, when you are not diplomatic enough you tend to say whatever is on your mind because you feel that it is your prerogative. Life doesn't work like that. We all need to learn how to edit ourselves. Speaking up is very important, but how you say it, when, to whom, and in what tone of voice are even more important. Your message can be confusing or imply the opposite of what you mean to say if you don't say it right. And sometimes — when you are not certain of the facts, for example — saying nothing at all is the right course of action. *Chismes* are never appropriate and only reflects negatively on the person transmitting it.

The 7 Strategies for the Savvy *Diplomática*

As a way to summarize the practical wisdom imparted in this chapter, I would like to offer you some simple strategies for becoming a better *diplomática*, based on the experiences of the inspiring Latina diplomats who have shared their stories with us. If you agree to the following seven statements — and commit to checking up on yourself periodically to see how well you are doing with them — I believe you will see that your relationships with people in both your professional and personal lives are going to improve.

1. *I will always speak in positive terms, avoiding name-calling and put-downs of others.*

    Lisa Fernández referred to this important principle when she talked about how she and her teammates communicate with and treat one another. Emphasizing the positive role that each member plays, while at the same time being able to give each other constructive advice, is a crucial aspect of their success as a team. And the same holds true for all of us, regardless of the type of team we are part of.

2. *I won't take the negative comments of others personally.*

    Remember the postcard Lisa was sent by someone who wanted to rub her nose in a game her Olympic team had lost? She said she "didn't take too kindly to that," but she ultimately thought of the incident as "motivation to push to be better." We enhance our Latina Power when we can accurately assess and learn from criticism, but also recognize that sometimes negative comments flung in our direction say more about who is flinging them than about us.

3. *I will cultivate my ability to be an open and respectful listener.*

    Both Congresswoman Loretta Sánchez and her sister, Congresswoman Linda Sánchez, were very insightful on this point. Listening with an open mind to the viewpoints of the other person is as important in our everyday lives—with our mates, our children, our friends, and our coworkers—as it is in the lives of political leaders and international negotiators. We can't understand, respect, or get along with others unless we listen to them authentically.

4. *I will seek to find common ground with those whose opinions differ from mine.*

    By learning to find common ground not only between workers and business owners but among the diverse cultures with whom she lived and worked in New York City, Dr. Antonia Pantoja was able to hone her *diplomática*'s skills. She continued to use this ability to benefit the struggling communities that needed her help. When we strive to do this as well, we can build a bridge between our own thinking and that of others with whom we disagree.

5. *I will learn the rules for becoming an insider in the field I want to enter.*

    Part of being a *diplomática* is learning to transform ourselves from an outsider to an insider, as María Pérez-Brown described earlier. And this process is about learning the rules so that others will accept you on their terms. Then, once you're an insider and have gained the trust of others and the experience you need, you can bend the rules that keep you from attaining your goals.

6. *I will be truthful yet respectful to myself and others.*

Too often people tend to think of being diplomatic as somehow skirting the issue or the truth. But as María Macías reminded us, diplomatically convincing someone who disagrees with you often entails very straightforward communication. In her case, she handled her husband's resistance to her going back to school with this simple, honest statement: "If you love me as I am, you will have to accept me as I am—and I'm going to school." For María, going to school is part of who she is. We can adapt to each other, but we cannot compromise the goals we need to reach in order to fulfill who we are. As *diplomáticas,* we need to listen respectfully to the differing opinions of others, but it is not our role to please them. Our role is to communicate honestly and respectfully with others while at the same time respecting our own ideas and goals.

7. *I will choose the right time, place, and tone in which to express my opinions.*

Nobody likes a complainer, but most people respect an honest, positive voice. As María Pérez-Brown pointed out, what distinguishes the two is diplomacy: "You learn to be diplomatic by seeing what the circumstances are and what the right timing will be to make a particular political stand." Choosing the appropriate moment, as well as the words and demeanor that will express your ideas without alienating the people you're communicating with, is no easy feat. But such *diplomacia* gets easier the more you use it.

6

The *Atrevida's* Courage

I always felt that I was supposed to do something different from my family, something bigger. At times I felt I was an alien in my own family. They sent me to Catholic school and I prayed a lot that I would be sent a sign about what direction I should take. We expect signs, but sometimes they appear in a form that's not too pleasant. . . .

When I was fourteen, I stood up for myself against the teachers in my school, who wrongly accused me of plagiarizing a creative story I had written. The incident blew up and there was an investigation and I did something that infuriated the school even more. But I could not put up with injustice. And I learned that if you know it's the right thing to do, and you take the risk, things happen that can change your life forever.

— Nely Galán, president,
Galan Productions

Throughout their history Latinos have had to courageously take risks. Some have had to leave their homeland and begin a new life in a foreign country so that their children could enjoy a safer or more promising future. Others have had to take risks in order to deal with difficult political or economic circumstances while at the same time keeping their families together. And as Latinas we sometimes have had to rebel against what our family or the church or our culture has told us is appropriate for women, in order to follow our own mission in life. With these various elements in our cultural background, it is no wonder that we have the guts and the energy to say "I'm going to be an *atrevida* and do what it takes to make my vision a reality." We can use this empowering trait to take productive risks that will further our personal goals.

In this chapter we will explore the fears that hold us back from realizing our true natures and accomplishing what we were meant to do. And we'll discover together how to interpret—even at times enjoy—our fearfulness, so that we can take the risks that are worthwhile and warranted but avoid the ones that are probably too harmful.

Harmony, Fear, and the Wisdom of the Toltecs

Being an *atrevida* is not only about taking risks. It's about looking at life as an adventure, creating new goals, and taking bold steps toward reaching those goals. Isn't our ultimate goal to live in harmony with who we are, with those we love, and with our environment? Spiritual guidance on how to live in harmony with the world is central to many religious and cultural traditions, including that of the Toltecs, whose culture flourished in Middle America a thousand years ago. The Toltecs believed in following a course by which one learns the truth about the world and oneself, as well as mastery over one's fears, so that a transformation of one's life energy can take place. This transformation—or spiritual growth, as we might call it today—results in being able to combine self-love and love for the world with the intent to live divinely or harmoniously within it. Key to this spiritual developmental process is the mastery of fear. According to the Toltecs, we need to overcome our fears in order to make the spiritual commitment to strive for our ideals and goals. Fearlessly discovering how to best use the talents and passions that life gives to each human being is part of this journey. As we begin to reach our goals, we get closer to merging our life's energy with that of the world's—and closer to a state of harmony.

So, as we learn to bring out the *atrevida* within ourselves, we can be inspired by the spiritual significance that the Toltecs attributed to dealing with fear. The less fearful we are the closer we will get to our life's mission, and the more in harmony we will be with ourselves and our world.

Confronting Our Fears

Fear, in its many forms, is the underlying reason we may doubt our ability to be a true *atrevida*. We may fear that our goals are not worth the struggle. Or that others will disapprove of our plans. Or we may be fearful that we won't survive on the risky new path we've chosen. Fear is not a bad thing. It often alerts us to real danger so that we can protect ourselves adequately. Perhaps we have decided to commit ourselves to a goal that is unsafe or unrealistic given our lack of preparation. Maybe we have a tendency to jump in and grab for every apparent opportunity that comes our way, even when our current abilities don't match up. If any of these are the case, we need to pay attention to what our fear is revealing to us and take steps to get the training or the education or the guidance that we need to stay on course with a particular goal. We can consider finding a mentor who is further along the same path and can help us diffuse the fear by enlightening us about what we need to do to better prepare ourselves. Or we might think about beginning at a level we feel more comfortable with, so that we dissipate our fear by accumulating the necessary expertise gradually.

Sometimes it's not a question of being unqualified or unprepared. We may be on an appropriate course but are beginning a new undertaking and simply fear the unknown. When we realize that this is what's fueling our fearfulness, we need to remind ourselves that a certain degree of apprehension is normal and can be overcome by acknowledging how well prepared we are as well as by networking with *comadres* who can provide us with the relevant insight and emotional support we need as we go down a new road.

Approaching new experiences with the attitude of an explorer is another useful technique in combating this common fear. If we can think of ourselves as being on the brink of discovering another piece of life's many delightful and bewildering mysteries, we become invested in the process of exploration rather than worried about failure or the risks of trying something new. In fact, the unknown aspects of everything we do are what turn life into a journey, as opposed to a treadmill. Doing the same thing over and over, like the poor little mouse on her caged wheel, assures our safety but not our growth. Once we break free from our cage and give ourselves over to exploring a new enterprise, we realize that the adventure and exhilaration of discovering something new always beats the safety of the treadmill.

What about the fear of disapproval? For many Latinas, being told that a particular path is not for women or not for Latinas inhibits their ability to stay committed to a goal they feel passionately about and that they are unquestionably qualified to achieve. Perhaps you unconsciously sabotage your success in a chosen field—telling yourself that Latinas should not become successful in this role or this career—in an effort to please your family or your husband or your community. Some fear that if they make certain changes that reflect an unconventional way of thinking, they will alienate themselves from their family or from others who love them. They fear that if they attain a level of accomplishment beyond that of their friends or family, or if they pursue aspirations that are different from their familys' and friends', those they love will shun them. So they end up sacrificing the possibility of new opportunities in order to maintain the status quo with those they love.

We can never be *atrevidas* if we feel that we are not entitled to pursue our dreams, and if we are sending ourselves self-sabotaging messages, we need to work on developing a sense of entitlement. For some Latinas, ties to their family or society are so strong that they need to detach themselves in order to disengage from the attitudes that have oppressed them, suffocated them, or not allowed them to be themselves. You don't necessarily have to move to another country or city to detach from an oppressive family or culture; sometimes this can take place within yourself. The process of disengaging involves learning to be unconcerned with *el qué dirán*. Learning to ignore the rejection and criticism of those who don't have your best interests at heart, who don't wish for you to become the woman you are capable of becoming, is part of the process of actualizing your *atrevida*.

Whatever the nature of your fear, becoming an *atrevida* entails truthfully confronting it, dealing with it by addressing the issues it raises, and then committing yourself wholeheartedly to the goals that reflect who you really are. Only you can be the one to select your goals; there is no way you can dedicate yourself passionately to a dream someone else has chosen for you. Certainly your objectives need to be realistic in terms of your education, skills, and training. But if you don't have the necessary qualifications, you can go after them. You can get the needed experience, information, education, or training. You can find out how others did it, find a mentor who will advise you, develop the new skills you'll need to begin your journey. Then, when you know that you are qualified to fulfill your goals, and that you passionately want to do so, your *atrevida's* courage will help you confront whatever fears arise.

Throughout this chapter we're going to discover that this process of self-confrontation, which transforms us into *atrevidas* of whom the Toltec would be proud, is neither harsh nor punishing, but rather an inner process of resolve and loving encouragement.

Sor Juana Inés de la Cruz
The Courage to Fly Against the Wind

If being an *atrevida* entails the courage to chart your own course despite the prevailing ideological winds, then certainly Sor Juana Inés de la Cruz, recognized as the first and most important literary figure in the New World, embodied the highest level of such *atrevimiento*. Born Juana Ramírez to an illiterate, unmarried woman around 1648 in New Spain (Mexico), Juana's first courageous act, unbeknownst to her mother, was to convince her older sister's tutor to also teach *her* how to read—even though she was only three years old. Juana soon took a keen interest in the many books in her grandfather's library, and by the time she was five or six her exceptional intelligence was apparent to everyone who knew her. As an older child she asked her mother if she might dress up as a boy in order to be able to attend the university. Although that never happened, Juana continued to study and to satisfy her intellectual curiosity on her own.

At the age of fifteen Juana became a lady-in-waiting at the court of the viceroy and vicereine of New Spain in Mexico City, where she impressed those who met her with her vast knowledge and sharp mind. She even overwhelmed a panel of professors who were sent to test her on subjects ranging from science, mathematics, and philosophy to theology and music. She far surpassed their expectations of what a woman might be capable of.

A turning point in Sor Juana's life came at the age of twenty, when she made the decision to become a nun. The rationale she gave years later revealed that her motivation for joining the convent was intellectual rather than religious. She wanted the freedom to study, write, and conduct scientific experiments—pursuits that women were not allowed to engage in at the time—and the convent was the only place she thought she might find it. While there, she wrote, among thousands of others, these poignant lines (from *Hombres Necios* ["Foolish Men"]) about men's hypocritical attitudes toward and treatment of prostitutes. For a woman to express herself in this way at that time was nothing short of audacious.

> Hombres necios que acusáis
> a la mujer sin razón,
> sin ver que sois la ocasión
> de lo mismo que culpáis:
>
> ¿O cuál es más de culpar,
> aunque cualquiera mal haga:

la que peca por la paga
o el que paga por pecar?

You foolish men, who accuse
Women without good reason,
You are the cause of what you blame,
Yours the guilt you deny.

When each is guilty of sin,
Which is the most to blame:
She who sins for payment,
Or he who pays for the sin? [1]

After twenty years of writing essays and poems, as well as of conducting research into the nature of knowledge, Sor Juana's probing
literary work was deemed too dangerous. Church officials prohibited
her from engaging in these activities further, her four thousand books
were confiscated, and she was forced to undertake a life of silence,
prayer, and physical penance. It seems that her ideas about women
being entitled to receive an education—to learn and to think—were in-
compatible with church and societal beliefs. Still, Sor Juana's life as
an intellectual and an *atrevida* serves as a testament to courage—the
courage to go against the powerful ideologies and institutions of her
day, not just for her own benefit, but on behalf of all women.

After decades of struggle, women in many countries today are afforded the kinds of freedoms and educational opportunities Sor Juana
would have treasured. When we think of the sacrifices she made and
the risks she took to educate herself and live her life as an intellectual—
enduring the scorn of the establishment, giving up a courtly life to live
in a convent, living as a nun—it can help us deepen our commitment to
developing our own intellectual potential.

1. From *Women, Culture, and Politics in Latin America,* by Emilie L. Bergmann, et al.,
Berkeley: University of California Press, 1992.

Dr. Sandra Milán
"I Get My *Atrevida* Courage From My Mother"

To engage in medical research you must be a risk taker. You must be open to exploring unproven possibilities and to dealing with unknown consequences. There is always the risk that your experiments will fail or that they will deliver unexpected or undesired results. But the process of searching for answers to important questions and problems is in itself assuredly worthwhile, as every scientist will attest. Dr. Sandra Milán is an *atrevida* who welcomes the risks of scientific research because she is committed to improving the health of people throughout the world. Most recently, she has been involved in the development of therapeutic treatments for breast cancer and non-Hodgkin's lymphoma and is currently in the process of obtaining clinical outcomes from a study she oversaw. It appears that those results are going to have a significant impact on the future of cancer treatment. The treatments do not involve a chemotherapy approach but rather enhance the patient's immune system with no—or very minor—side effects.

How did a woman born in Guadalajara, Mexico, and raised by a single mother of seven children, wind up with a doctorate from the University of California, Berkeley, and go on to become a medical researcher on the brink of a discovery that could change the way patients are treated for cancer? When I talked to Sandra about some of the motivating influences in her family life, she told me that, being the youngest of seven, she had to learn how to be smart within her family. And she looked to her mother as a role model: "I had to compete with my siblings, gain attention, struggle to understand what was going on with everyone else, and master my communication skills to explain what I wanted. I get my *atrevida* courage from my mother, because she had to raise all of us as a single parent, and the job was daunting. I learned from her how to roll up my sleeves, and if I can't get the outcome I desire, I learn from the experience and keep going. I keep moving forward."

Sandra also may have been influenced by her mother's career in the health field; in addition to being mom to seven kids, she has a nursing degree from Mexico that is similar to one for a licensed vocational nurse (LVN) here. Sandra's family came to San Francisco, California, when Sandra was fourteen, and adjusting to the new culture was often jarring: "I went through growing pains in high school in the Bay Area. As a teenager, I didn't want to come to the U.S. I didn't speak the language, so it wasn't easy. In fact, it was really traumatic for me. I didn't know the neighbors, I didn't know the school, I couldn't even relate to the kids because of the language thing. So the first two years were incredibly hard for me. I lived in isolation."

After high school Sandra initially went to a state college and then transferred to the University of California, Santa Cruz, where there was a large number of minority students but few women in the various science programs. Although she knew she loved science, she had to assess her strengths and weaknesses candidly before she could embark on a specific career path. She was fortunate to have a number of devoted mentors at Santa Cruz who were very supportive and really wanted to see minority students develop into scientists. Both her professors and fellow students—most of whom were male—gave her great motivation and drive. Although she always had been very analytical and scientifically oriented, at first she didn't know which career direction she wanted to go in. "I wasn't particularly good at memorization, so I decided *not* to go to medical school. But I knew I had good analytical skills and enjoyed being involved in research projects, so I made a decision to go into a Ph.D. program in molecular biology at U.C. Berkeley."

Another important influence in Sandra's life, in addition to her *atrevida* mother and the mentors who encouraged her in college, has been her interest in Latino history. She told me that on her path toward becoming a medical researcher the scientists who inspired her most were those from the early native cultures of Mexico and Latin America. "A sense of history is critical to understanding where you're going,

where you come from, and who your heroes are," she says. "I'm proud
to be a Mexicana. To understand the native Indian cultures of Mexico
and Latin America and the scientific contributions they made—that's
very important to me. The Aztec calendar, the Mayan astronomy and
architecture, the stonemasonry, medical surgery, and medicinal cures
of the Incas—knowing about those discoveries and the richness of
those cultures gives me the goose bumps."

Sandra recognizes her *atrevida* roots not only in her immediate
family but in her historical family as well—in the early civilizations of
Mexico and South America. She told me she is so inspired by the scientific breakthroughs of the Aztecs, Maya, and Incas that she is motivated to make her own research relevant to as many people as possible.
"Realizing that what those cultures contributed has had a ripple effect
throughout the centuries—that's what motivates me. Their scientists
had an impact hundreds and hundreds of years later. And I want to
have that kind of impact. I think we can all make a contribution, not
only to the community, but to the world."

Sandra's mission is to continue her research so that people's quality of life—and the health of the world—is improved. Her unofficial
motto is "Love what you do, but know your limits. Never commit to
what you cannot deliver." The important work she does has involved
much risk-taking, including the move to a foreign country, the pursuit
of a traditionally male career, and the uncertainty inherent in scientific
experimentation. But her research is her gift to the world—delivered
with passion, commitment, and love.

Nely Galán
Entertainment Executive y *Peleonera*

Regarded as one of the entertainment industry's most dynamic creative executives, Nely Galán has dedicated her career to making
television more relevant for Latinos and to putting more Latinos on
television. She is president of Galan Productions and executive pro-

ducer of Telemundo's *Sólo en América, Los Beltrán,* and *Padre Alberto.* Her producing credits also include the telenovela *Empire,* the new sitcom *Viva Vegas,* and the Bravo Awards honoring achievements of Latinos in entertainment. Dubbed the "Tropical Tycoon" and the "Cuban Missile" by *The New York Times Magazine,* Nely considers herself a warrior. And in the entertainment business perhaps that is the role one most needs to assume, especially if you are a Latina.

Nely was born in Cuba and immigrated with her family to New Jersey at the age of two. She began her media career as an editor at *Seventeen* magazine, but she didn't simply apply for the job. She got the magazine's attention by being an intelligently outspoken *atrevida.* When we spoke Nely told me the story behind her first job—and about her personal transformation from a shy teenager into a daring *peleonera.*

"When I was fourteen years old my whole life changed forever," she said, "and it all started with a creative writing assignment. I wrote a story about an older woman about to die who looks back on her life and what she has learned. Even though my teacher gave me an A, the nuns at the Catholic school I was attending didn't believe I had written the story. I told them, 'Listen, my parents are immigrants and I can see how life is. I'm already an old person at heart—that's why I could create that story.' "

Still, Nely was accused of plagiarism, which angered her so much that she wrote an article called "Why Parents Shouldn't Send Their Kids to Catholic School" and sent it to *Seventeen* magazine. Not only was the article published, but *Seventeen* asked her to become a teenage editor. "My parents called me *loca* and sacrilegious, the nuns accused me of being an Hispanic with a chip on my shoulder, and the school threatened to expel me for writing the article. But standing up for myself, I became a *peleonera,* a warrior. I went from being a quiet and shy little girl to being totally in power. I learned from this incident that if you take the risk, you can create change. My sense of injustice forced me to take action—and that action became my metamorphosis."

Nely took action against the injustice done to her not only by sending her story to *Seventeen* magazine; when the school threatened to expel her for writing the article, she took her grievance to the school board. She met with a member of the board and asked him, "Can the nuns expel me for writing an article?" He told her, "Of course not." So the school board investigated the incident, invoked the First Amendment, and the school settled her case out of court. Nely graduated a year and a half early, and her career as a media *atrevida* was under way.

After her stint at *Seventeen* Nely was recruited by Norman Lear and Jerry Perenchio to manage the Spanish-language television station WNJU-TV, Telemundo's flagship station in Linden, New Jersey. At twenty-two, Nely became the youngest television station manager in the United States. She went on to head up both HBO and Fox Latin America's Latino programming divisions, as well as Telemundo's entertainment division.

Producing a talk show featuring a hip, Catholic priest *(Padre Alberto)* and a drama featuring a divorced mom with a full-time job *(Sólo en América)*, so unlike the telenovelas often seen on Spanish-language stations, is evidence of Nely's willingness to take creative risks. Why are courage and risk-taking so important for a Latina in the competitive entertainment industry? It is very unusual for a woman—let alone a Latina—to achieve the kind of success as a television producer that Nely has. Although she has been accused of being aggressive, she really is just very, very assertive—and a true *atrevida!* This is a woman who gains access to places of power where few others can. She focuses on what she wants to do and goes at it fearlessly. There is no one in the Spanish-speaking television market today who has her brand of daring. She fights for what she believes in, digs in her heels, and keeps taking the risks until she achieves her vision. For this warrior *atrevida*, the word "impossible" only intensifies her bravery.

Dr. Elvia Niebla
A Seven-Year-Old Latina Superman, a Pink Dog, and Zero Barriers

Like fellow scientist Sandra Milán, Elvia Niebla was inspired early on by her mother to dream big and to reach beyond the expected roles for Latinas. Her mom instilled in her the exhilarating sense that absolutely anything is possible if you are determined and courageous enough. And she didn't just talk the talk — she exemplified that *atrevida* spirit in everything she did. While being Mom to her four children in Nogales, Mexico, she also won the admiration of the many families in that town whose lives she touched. Elvia spoke warmly and with pride of her mother's achievements in those early days.

"When I was little, I admired my mother, because there was nothing she couldn't do," Elvia recalled. "Whatever she proposed to do, she just went ahead and did it. And that's the image I have of her, that she was a true *atrevida*. She made *pasteles muy buenos*, she could do perms and cut hair, and she was also a midwife. She worked in a special clinic with a doctor, and she would stay with a new mother for three days — twenty-four hours a day — after the baby was born. So many people in Nogales loved her because of the work that she did." There was one occasion in particular that Elvia remembers, when a woman about to deliver her baby called to say she was on the way to the clinic. When she arrived in the taxi she was already giving birth, and since the doctor had not yet arrived, Elvia's mother helped this woman give birth inside the taxi.

"I was always fascinated by what my mother could do," Elvia said, "and I learned from her that nothing is impossible. The main thing was to work hard, but to also love what you do. What I saw in her was that she always had fun doing whatever she was involved in."

Elvia's sense of being able to make things happen — her belief in her ability to turn what others might think is an outrageous idea into reality — was nurtured by her mother through play when Elvia was growing up. How many moms fifty years ago would have encouraged their daughters to dress up like a male superhero? (This was, after all, decades before women's lib and *Superwoman* were part of our cultural landscape.) And how many parents would give in to their child's fantasy in order to create a bit of magic with the family pet? Elvia's mom was definitely an *atrevida* role model. "Whatever I had in mind, my mom would look for a way to help me make it happen," Elvia told me. "Rather than saying I couldn't do something that might be harmful, she would help me find a way to do it anyway, a safe way. I remember when I was seven, I wanted to play Superman. So my mother made me a cape and created that image for me. And at that time I felt that I really could be like Superman. Because she allowed me to feel this way, that was how I thought of myself."

Another time, Elvia decided that she wanted to color her dog pink. Rather than tell her daughter this was a silly or impractical idea, her mom said, "Well, we can't actually dye his fur, but we can do it with food coloring." So they gave the dog a color job, painted his nails, and he turned out just as Elvia had hoped he would: bright, bright pink! "My mom went along with it — and that's the sense I got from her, that you can do whatever you envision, that there's always a way to get around obstacles."

Elvia's mom also used her *atrevida's* courage to make the decision to move with her children to the United States when her oldest child was unable to further his education in Mexico. In her new home in Nogales, Arizona, Elvia soon became one of the best students in her school. However, as a Chicana, she was advised by the teachers there to choose a different career than the one she had in mind. Although she always had liked science and research in school, she was encouraged to become a Spanish teacher — because that was the direction in which smart Chicanas were guided. "But I didn't want to do that," Elvia recalled. "I wanted to be a scientist!"

Again, her mother was there providing Elvia with the encouragement to take the risk, go against the grain, and do whatever she wanted to do. So Elvia took the science program in high school, got her bachelor's degree in zoology (with a minor in chemistry) from the University of Arizona, Tucson, completed a master's degree in special education ("because I wanted to teach science to the physically handicapped"), and ultimately got her Ph.D. in soil chemistry. Throughout her university education her classes were comprised almost entirely of men. As is still the case today—although more women are now entering those fields—women were a rarity in the sciences: "In a class of forty, only two or three would be women, and there were no Chicanos. I always knew that I had to be the best; I couldn't be mediocre."

Elvia is anything but. Today she lives in Washington, D.C., and works at the highest level studying and combating environmental pollution. She is the national coordinator of the Global Change Research Program for the U.S. Forest Service and oversees 180 scientists doing research to determine the impact environmental chemicals have on global climate change.

Throughout her life Elvia has used the *atrevida* spirit she inherited from her mother to fearlessly pursue whatever she envisions, whether it's challenging world governments to change their environmental policies, entering academic programs previously unattended by Chicanas, soaring like a superhero where only boys were supposed to fly—or painting her dog the electrifying color she dreamed of.

Olga Marta Peña Doria
Shining the Spotlight on Mexican "Women of Disobedience"

Sometimes being an *atrevida* requires that we defy the status quo in order to realize our vision. Throughout history women have had to break rules in order to make their voices heard, and Latinas are no exception. While stories about courageous women who broke the mold do not always make the pages of mainstream history books, it is wonderful when we can discover those who paved the way for us.

A professor of theater at the University of Guadalajara, Olga

Doria's mission has been to celebrate in writing the *heroínas mexicanas* of the 1920s and 1930s who bravely gave a voice to Mexican women's struggle for equality. These were women working in the theater at an important time in Mexican history, because the revolution had ended and women were beginning to speak out about their right to vote, to get an education, and to be treated more fairly. No woman in Mexico since Sor Juana Inés de la Cruz, who was considered the country's first feminist, had addressed women's rights publicly, and the theater was one of the settings in which such risky subjects could be explored. Mexican women found in the theater of that time the feminine models they needed to fuel their dream of liberation. Women playwrights of this era offered female characters who were in stark contrast to *la madre sufrida, la abnegada,* etc., namely, women who were either professionals (mainly medical doctors and attorneys) or had enough money to be able to make their own decisions.

One writer highlighted in Olga's book *Digo Yo Como Mujer, Catalina D'Erzell* (Nuestra Cultura, 2000, Mexico), D'Erzell herself, is among the first women in Mexico to become a media figure. She wrote a column entitled *"Digo Yo Como Mujer"* ("As a Woman I Say") for a number of major Mexican newspapers, as well as radio scripts, novels, short stories, poetry, opera, and plays. In her twelve plays she addressed the issues of honor and dishonor, passion, *unión libre* (living with someone outside marriage), and divorce—a word that women didn't even dare contemplate at that time. But D'Erzell was indeed daring, and her plays were very successful. For the first time in the history of Mexico, women were the ones filling the seats of the theater. And thus this period became known as "The Disobedience of the 1920s and 1930s."

So Olga refers to the women of this period as "women of disobedience," another of whom was Amalia de Castillo Ledon, a successful playwright who also tackled the taboo subject of divorce. Her play highlighting this issue, the first written by a woman to have a public performance, features a conflict between a mother and daughter, in which the mother suggests that the daughter divorce her husband.

Although this was a highly disrespectful and antiestablishment idea at the time, the play enjoyed one hundred performances. Amalia was also a political activist. She traveled throughout Latin America campaigning on behalf of the vote for women. Her efforts proved successful in seventeen countries, but it wasn't until 1953 that they finally paid off in Mexico. On December 28, 1952, Amalia went to the Mexican Congress and spoke in favor of the vote for women. On January 1, 1953, the right of women to vote was signed into law, and Amalia was there in Congress to give a speech thanking them for this historic victory for women. She went on to hold the first position in the government as the Sub-Secretaria de Cultura in 1953, under President Adolfo López Mateos.

Olga talked to me about the frustration that initially led her to write a book about these groundbreaking *atrevidas*. "Did you know that they didn't put Amalia de Castillo Ledon in any book of history of the theater?" she asked me. "Only men. So I kept asking myself, Why is that? Why did they forget about these women? Why are they not given the celebrity they deserve? And I realized that such women have been referred to as lesbians, prostitutes, dumb — but never recognized as intellectuals, which is what they were." So Olga decided that she was going to be another *atrevida*, another "disobedient one" and write about them. "Everybody laughed about my idea for this book, told me that it was not important, that these women only wrote melodramas, and that their contributions to the theater were ridiculous. They didn't realize that these playwrights were waking up the consciousness of women."

Initially, Olga had difficulty researching the lives of these important "disobedient" women. Although she was able to track down their daughters, granddaughters, and other relatives, many of them did not trust her, because she was an unknown person to them. But Olga was tenacious, refusing to be deterred from her mission to tell the life stories of Mexico's innovative feminist playwrights. She persisted in the face of the untrusting relatives, her skeptical colleagues, and a number of pessimistic publishers—and now her book inspires readers with one of the richest periods of women's liberation history.

There is also a sad part to Olga's story. She told me that while she is proud of her triumph in publishing her latest book, there are still many young women who seem to be oblivious to the lessons it imparts. When she asks her female students why they are taking her class, many respond "I am only going to college while I wait to get married." Olga is very disappointed in such statements, because they reveal that young women still need to develop themselves to the point where their ultimate goal reaches beyond becoming a *reina del hogar.*

Too Much Risk . . . Or Not Enough?

Confronting our fears in order to become courageous *atrevidas* is an important facet of empowering ourselves. Unless we're prepared to risk the unknown, the dangerous, the unpredictable, we can't ever create change in our lives, but we need to be careful about how far we take our fearlessness. I invite you now to think about whether your approach to the challenges you face on your path to fulfilling your vision might be either too risky or not risky enough.

If you tend to leap before you look, you probably pay a price. You may indeed find yourself over your head in terms of being unprepared or vulnerable to too many hardships or hazards. If this is the case, you need to pay more attention to the risks associated with your particular venture and the alternative options you might have overlooked. Is this the best time to be plunging into your project—or might it be better to wait until the external circumstances are more favorable or until you've done more planning? Have you evaluated the potential consequences of your action wisely—or are you so stirred by your vision that you have thrown *demasiado* caution to the wind?

When we take a risk, we often have to give up something in order to gain something else. Perhaps it is a way of life or money or security. Sometimes it may even be the moral support of your family, which is a big issue with Latinas. If it's possible that you may alienate your family by taking a risk that is untraditional, it is important to take that into consideration before making a decision. We shouldn't ignore such risks, but we shouldn't hold ourselves back because of them either.

On the other hand, you can't set your dreams in motion by standing still and clinging fearfully to the status quo. You have to join the dance. When you always seem to be waiting for somebody else to make the first move, it's a sign that your *atrevida* is asleep inside you and needs to be awakened. You can't expect a politician to consider your community's needs unless you risk getting involved and making her or him understand what those needs are. You can't assume that your child's teacher is addressing a learning problem unless you take a proactive role. And you can't just hope that your employer will one day give you the raise you deserve—you have to let him or her know about the great job you are doing.

If you take only safe steps on the way to your goals, chances are you'll never fulfill your potential. Rather, you'll be like a child with an overprotective mother, listening only to your cautious inner voice and perpetuating the myth that women are the *sexo débil*. So why not start experimenting with an *atrevida's* attitude by telling yourself *"Sí, se puede"* and picturing yourself breaking free from the status quo cage you may have erected unknowingly? Where do you venture off to and what expressive dance do you perform when you give yourself this new freedom?

Enjoying the Fear of Creative Risk-Taking

Sometimes being an *atrevida* means feeling your fear and actually enjoying it. Enjoying the exciting feeling, which comes from knowing that you're trying something new and that your effort is meaningful and pleasing to you—even if it might ultimately fail. Before I appear on my radio and TV shows or give a workshop, I usually feel a sense of tension. Although that kind of nervousness can paralyze some people,

I find that for me it creates an excitement. It tells me that I'm about to do something that is important to me and to others, which is a tremendous sense of responsibility. When I first opened my practice, I would worry about how a new patient might respond to what I would say. However, with time and experience, I not only became more confident of my abilities, I also learned to think about fear in terms of excitement. This kind of fear/excitement is a by-product of engaging in life rather than withholding yourself from it—and for that reason it can be very enjoyable.

The thrill of taking a creative risk—whether you're a television producer, a scientist, or a preschool teacher—can be its own reward. When we're open to enjoying uncharted territory, we become explorers with the confidence and curiosity to encounter new opportunities. Fear is part of the journey, but it is very closely related to delight and excitement. So who says fear has to be your enemy? Maybe the two of you just need to get together and talk—and understand each other better.

Your *Atrevida* Talks Openly to Your Fears—A Dialogue Exercise

As we have been saying throughout this chapter, there is nothing wrong with acknowledging your fears; in fact, some of them may be protecting you from acting unwisely or taking risks for which you're unprepared. But once you've set realistic goals, made necessary preparations, and are sure of the direction in which you want to be headed, it would be a waste to allow your fears to keep you from what you want to do with your life—especially when you have the potential for being a gutsy *atrevida*. We've learned about the ways in which Latinas tend to inherit an *atrevida*'s courage—through our parents' struggles, our own life experiences, and an awareness of the spiritual significance of mastering fear in the native cultures of Latin America. So now let's imagine these two aspects of ourselves—our *atrevida* and our fears—having a rational yet spirited conversation.

After you read the sample dialogue below, try writing your own — and see what you discover about who has the upper hand.

ATREVIDA: I say we go for it! We've been wanting to (try out for that play, apply for that small business loan, get into that master's degree program) for months now. So what's holding us back?

FEARS: I'll tell you what's holding us back! We're unqualified! And as much as you might try to convince me that we have enough going for us to "go for it," I'm not budging. I don't want us to fall flat on our face.

ATREVIDA: You say we're unqualified, and yet we've already laid the groundwork for this next step. All we have to do is take the risk! And if we fall? What's the big deal about getting up and trying again?

FEARS: Humiliation, for one. And besides, this is something that (my parents, my husband, my friends, my relatives) disapprove of. I don't want to disappoint them or make them feel uncomfortable.

ATREVIDA: So you're going to sacrifice the chance to become the woman we were meant to be — and throw away the gifts we were born with and the skills we've developed — just so *los otros* won't feel uncomfortable?

FEARS: But we might stand out too much from the crowd if we become too successful — and then no one will love us!

ATREVIDA: What about loving ourselves? And what better way to show it than — going for it!

Atrevida Visualization Exercise

Now that you've heard what your fears are telling you, this second exercise will help you to relax as you gather the confidence to deal with them. You might want to record the following onto a cassette tape, so that the exercise will be easier to do.

Select a quiet place where you won't be interrupted by anyone. Sit in a comfortable chair or lie down on a bed, a couch, or the floor. Relax and begin to calm your body completely by taking slow, deep breaths. We're going to take a peaceful journey inward.

Let your mind transport you to a place where you have felt secure in the past. This might be a place that is real or one that is imaginary. You are now in this place, and you feel very comfortable. You are enjoying being in this beautiful, soothing environment. You appreciate its beauty with all your senses. You enjoy its smell, the feel of the breeze, or the sun, or the light rain on your face, the peaceful sounds in the air, the pleasing colors. You are now in a setting that is completely comforting.

Now remember a recent fear or one from your past. Bring this fear into your consciousness and try to feel it as you did the last time it appeared in your life. Relive the way you felt when you were last confronted by this fear. Go beyond just remembering it and actually try to re-experience that fear. Visualize all the negative feelings which this fear brings up. Pay attention to what you are feeling now, both in your body and in your mind.

Now come up with an image that symbolizes this fear for you. This image might be an object, an animal, a mythological or cartoon character—anything that accurately represents this fear. Have you selected your image? Good.

Now observe this image of fear very, very carefully, so that you familiarize yourself with its every characteristic. Now you can actually see this fearful image so clearly that you can take it into your hands and speak to it. Ask it, "Why are you there in my mind? What is your reason for existing within me? What kind of danger do you want to protect me from?" This symbol in your hands will now answer you. Give yourself the time to listen to its response.

You realize that the intention of this fear, of this image, is good. But it may also be excessively threatening. You are grateful for its presence, but you can now tell it that you have the ability to live a safe life, to protect yourself without paralyzing yourself, and therefore don't need its presence in your mind any longer.

Now take a look around you in this comforting environment that you have created in your mind. Notice that you feel peaceful and safe. Realize that this peace and safety are within you—and that you bring this tranquility and safety with you wherever you go.

Now tell that symbol of fear goodbye—and let it go. The symbol leaves your hand, drifts away from you, and you are happy that it has left you. Because you know that the peace and security that you have just created are yours to keep. They will accompany you today and always, because you now have a greater awareness of who you are, what you may do or become without restricting yourself, and a more realistic sense of what your fear represents.

And now, slowly come back to where you are in the room. Focus on your breathing, and on every part of your body, feeling every part of your body to be very alive. Open your eyes and acknowledge your environment. Keep the peace and security that you have just created alive within you. They're yours.

7

The *Malabarista*'s Balance

The main goal of the Aztecs is to live in harmony with this universe, of which they are a part. They believe that the universe is made up of an immense net of energy channels that meet and combine at different points. If everything is in balance, what they refer to as supreme equilibrium exists.

—Elena Avila, *Woman Who Glows in the Dark*

As Latinas we learn from our families and our culture about the need to balance our numerous responsibilities: to our parents, spouse, children, extended families, communities, and spiritual life. And we seem to take this requirement in stride. Women in general and Latinas in particular have a highly developed ability to be effective "multitaskers" and to balance many different pursuits concurrently. Although it can be daunting, we always seem to find a way to be the *malabarista* and to deftly manage everything on our plate. Nowadays many of us have added a vital element to our balancing act: our own goals, be they a higher education, a career, or a talent we want to develop. In this chapter we're going to talk about how to accomplish the challenging task of creating balance in our lives so that we have the energy and the time to devote to the pursuits and the people that are most important to us, including ourselves.

We also are going to explore what it means to have a sense of inner balance, whereby we give caring attention to the various aspects of our selves that make us feel fully alive and vital. When we achieve this kind of balance, we can approach what Elena Avila describes as the Aztec sense of "supreme equilibrium."

Throughout this chapter you'll meet some exemplary *malabaristas* who will share their secrets and strategies for leading a balanced life, for enjoying their families, their professional pursuits and other interests that define who they are.

Devoted to Two Worlds
TV Journalist María Elena Salinas

Emmy Award–winning television journalist María Elena Salinas didn't always know she wanted a career in journalism, but even as a young girl she was motivated to think in terms of having both *familia y trabajo* in her future, due to the positive example her mother had provided. She told me that she never felt slighted as a child whose mom worked outside the home. And although her family needed her mother's income, María says she had no idea that they were poor because she felt so loved and taken care of. "I never thought about becoming a reporter, but I always thought about doing something that would give pride to my parents," she said. "I was very close to my parents, especially to my mom. She always worked, but I never lacked for either her attention or her love. So I always thought about having the same things for myself one day—my own family and a career."

As a young teenager in Los Angeles, María Elena held down jobs in a clothing factory, a cafeteria, and a movie theater and helped pay for her Catholic school education. Unsure at first what career would be best suited to her interests and talents, María considered becoming a fashion designer and later attended community college to study marketing for the fashion industry. In her early twenties she worked at a community center teaching women from very poor backgrounds about self-esteem, fashion, and grooming. A friend who worked with her at the center also worked at a radio station and introduced María Elena to a producer, who soon recruited her to do news and music programs. After advancing to production director at the radio station and taking additional courses in journalism at UCLA, María Elena was offered a job as a reporter and talk show host with Channel 34, the Los Angeles affiliate of the Spanish International Network, which later became Univision.

Her rise up the media ladder continued, as did María Elena's commitment to serving her community and covering socially relevant stories. Over the years María Elena has interviewed every president in Latin America, as well as Mexican Zapatista leader Sub-Comandante Marcos. She also has found the time to become involved in Radio Unica's campaign to encourage Latino students to stay in school and in a number of drives to get out the vote in Hispanic communities.

Drawing information and insight from world leaders and contributing her time to important social causes is never *más importante*, however, than being an involved mom with her two young daughters, Julia and Gabriela. On María Elena's website, you can click on a section called *"Familia"* and discover her concern for the balance that working moms strive for. She states in that section: "I believe that sharing my experiences as a woman, mother and wife, as well as a journalist, can help to create a dialogue among women who, like me, have to divide themselves between two worlds—the professional and personal. I would love it if the readers of this section would share with me their own experiences of *'mamá profesional.'*"

So how does María Elena manage to inhabit these two worlds in such a way that she can derive fulfillment from both? As any of us who work and have young children know, it usually isn't easy. But María Elena was determined to make working motherhood work. She told me that when she had her daughters she already had a career and a societal commitment—and didn't want to give those up. "I'm a communicator, and I could never see myself dropping that." Although it used to break her heart when her younger daughter, Gabriela, pleaded with her in the mornings not to go to work, she kept reminding herself of several important realities: that her income helps to assure that both her daughters will have a good education; that Gabriela was flourishing in preschool; and that her girls know their mom is always there for them. "Gabrielita learned things going to preschool that she could not learn being at home alone with her mom," she said, "like socialization, sharing with others, defending her rights and respecting the rights of others. If I thought that my daughters would be worse human beings because I work, then I wouldn't think about it twice; I would change my lifestyle completely. My daughters miss me sometimes, but they know that they have me. The first thing they see in the morning and the last thing they see at night is their mom. At work I call them on the phone, and they tell me things and I tell them things—so we keep up a lively communication throughout the day."

As María Elena explained to me, her husband, Cuban-American news anchor Elliott Rodríguez, is another big reason she can maintain the balance between family and career. Her husband cooks, and he's the one who makes sure that dinner is ready every night. Also, they have a schedule for who's going to do the grocery shopping—sometimes they do it separately and sometimes together. "We both have to work at scheduling everything into our agendas," she says, "but we have it all organized, including what we're going to do on the weekends, when we're going to do our errands, when we're going to spend time together as a couple or with our children. My husband likes to have one day with each child separately, when he takes each daughter to ride her bike or go to the bookstore or play tennis. He also spends time with his older children, my stepchildren. Being with our children as much as possible is extremely important to both of us."

Although they devote lots of time to their children on the weekends, María Elena and Elliott also still make dates together as a couple, taking advantage of the nightlife in Miami, where they live. And during the week they manage to squeeze in a few lunch dates as well. Sounds romantic, no? María Elena is grateful that as busy as they both are, and as devoted as they continue to be to their careers and their children, she and her husband still value and enjoy their relationship: "It's not just work and children. After the girls go to sleep, we take time for ourselves."

María Elena admits that maintaining a balance among work, social service, children, and spouse involves being an ace organizer. But she remains as dedicated as ever to a career that she continues to find exhilarating. Although her life is full, she says she always looks forward to new projects "because I don't want to become a *conformista*, someone who's comfortable with the status quo. I love my job, and I want to do it better all the time."

When Your Mate Can't Handle Your Success

Some of you may be thinking that María Elena Salinas's life sounds a little too good to be true, especially when it comes to her very supportive husband and their romantic connection as a couple. Although her story is indeed a true one, there are many Latinas whose working lives cause serious issues and problems for their mates. As Latinas continue to make strides in the workplace, our husbands or boyfriends are being called upon to make adjustments in their own attitudes and behavior, and we need to confront the stresses that can be placed on a couple's relationship when a woman has a career outside the home. There's no way we can enjoy a sense of balance in our lives when our most significant relationship is tense or problematic.

Interestingly, what I found in interviewing successful Latinas for this book was that those who are married and reside in Latin America told me they have very supportive partners, which they appreciate very much. Their husbands are, of course, Latinos. I was surprised to discover, however, that most of the married Latinas in the United States whom I interviewed are married to non-Latinos. And the reason they gave for why that is the case is that, according to them, they were not able to find a Latino husband who could support them emotionally in their careers. Of course there are successful Latinas in the United States married to supportive Latino men (I am one of them!), but we have to take a look at why so many Latinas can't seem to find the right Latino mates.

We are going through a period of rapid social change throughout the West, but the process men must go through to adapt to such changes in their women can take time. Although the women's movement of the 1960s and 70s is already more than thirty years old, roles for Latino women and men are still in a state of flux, and this shift is particularly challenging for some Latino men. They ask themselves "If I'm not the sole breadwinner anymore, or the one who makes all the important decisions, then who am I?" At the same time, many Latinas were taught never to shine more than their husbands *("No hacerle sombra")* because if they do the men might feel emasculated. And yet, more and more women are shining nonetheless, and some are suffering the resentment of their partners as a result. So how do you ensure a healthy, loving relationship with your man while at the same time enjoying your own life and your own accomplishments?

First of all, it's important to get to the bottom of why the man in your life might resent your quest for success or your involvement in the world outside of your home. Does he still believe that a *mujer's* place is *en el hogar?* Does he feel ignored by you now that you're pursuing a career? Is it possible that he feels threatened by the fact that you make more money than he does, or that your job is more prestigious than his?

He might resent you because he's not yet used to the image of a woman who is outgoing and successful. That might be threatening to him not only because it's a change from what he grew up with but also because he may have gotten the message somewhere in his family or the culture that women's success may lead to the breakup of the relationship or that as a result they will not pay enough attention to their husbands or children. Some men are very demanding of their wives' attention—they even get jealous when children are born—so for them also to have to compete with their wives' careers makes it even harder for them.

With regard to money, some men from a very traditional Latino culture can feel insecure about their wives earning an income, or a larger income than they do. This can throw into question a man's sense of masculinity. Unfortunately, we're usually still measured by how much money we make, and if a wife makes more than her husband, she's considered more successful, so he may think that others perceive him as not as capable as she is. Men are trained to feel proud of what they do, to be *un hombre de bien;* however, if your wife or girlfriend gets more attention than you do, some men may feel that they're not measuring up. Many Latino men want to be the focus of attention, and when they're not, their pride suffers.

In my own life, sometimes I am considered the "wife of" Alex Nogales, president and CEO of the National Hispanic Media Coalition. But at other times, he is the "husband of" Dr. Ana Nogales. He responds very well to that, and feels very proud of who I am and what I do, but not all men would, because not all men feel proud to be "the spouse of," which is of course the way women traditionally have been described. Being described as the "spouse of" can feel as if you are being put in second place, and Latino men especially think of themselves as the head of the family.

What to do about these resentments? If the issue is about time and he feels you are giving less of it to him now that you are busy with your job or career, understand that this shift in your life may have created an imbalance in your relationship. Try to see the situation from his perspective. Traditionally, women have been on that side of the fence, upset that their husbands were so busy with their careers that they didn't have enough time with them and their children. Whether it's the man or the woman making the argument, too much time away from your partner and family creates a distance in your relationship. If this is the case, you might want to make adjustments in your schedule so that you regain some of that time.

As women we tend to be more able to express our feelings, so we can say, "You know, I wish we could spend more time together. I miss you, and I miss the time when I used to come home every night and we could take a walk, tell each other about our day, and fix dinner together." What I've seen with my clients is that men won't say these kinds of things, but instead they will act resentful because their wives are not there. So maybe you will have to be the one to open up the discussion and offer possible solutions.

Another suggestion: Find a way to involve him somehow in your work or pursuit. If you're going back to school, invite him to come with you one night. If you're starting a new business, find a way to have him participate so he understands why this enterprise is important to you. That inclusion will make him feel more accepting of the changes that are happening.

And finally, we have to consider that our men are not perfect. They have their own issues that may determine how they react to our success. For example, I have patients who have a history of being abandoned, either by a parent or another relationship. And for this reason their feelings of abandonment are activated when their wife or girlfriend spends less time with them. Other men may have experienced betrayal in a previous relationship or marriage, so that when their wives are dressing up and getting ready to go to a meeting where other men will be around, those feelings of betrayal resurface. I have a patient whose mother died from cancer at an early age and he has therefore always had a strong need to be nurtured. He needs the consistent presence of a woman, and had that for many years with his wife, but now that she is changing her life, he's not ready for it.

It's not always easy for the men we love to change with us as we are making changes to enhance our lives. We need to learn how to encourage such change in our partners so that our relationship benefits and each of us feels free to grow.

My *Mami,* the Scientist
Biology Professor Leticia Márquez-Magaña

Innovative researcher, professor, and mentor, mom to two young sons, and wife of a pediatrician, San Francisco State University professor

Leticia Márquez-Magaña says she owes her success in part to her mother and to her *abuelas*. She told me that when Latinas hear the *abuela* stories of their grandmothers who were unable to do things because of economic or social limitations, they are inspired to accomplish what their *abuelas* could not. The dramatic stories in Leticia's own family history motivated her to focus intently on creating a fulfilling life as a scientist.

Her family's *historia de las mujeres* went something like this: Leticia's *tatarabuela*, whose parents came from Spain and owned a *rancho* in Mexico, was forced to marry an indigenous man who had raped her. Her great-grandmother ran away with her lover to get married. Her grandmother had wanted to explore the world but instead got married at age fifteen and died at thirty-six after giving birth to thirteen children. And her mother, the oldest of the thirteen, desperately wanted to go to school but was only able to finish two months of the second grade. Still, she was so interested in learning and in teaching that she became a teacher to the other children on the *rancho*. Coming from this long line of dashed hopes Leticia promised herself—and the women who preceded her in her family—that she indeed would fulfill her own potential and make her own dreams a reality.

"From my family stories, I learned that it was up to me to empower myself with education," she told me. "It was also a way of healing what my family had been unable to do in terms of their education. My dad was born on *el rancho* too. In order to be able to go to school, he went into the seminary system. But he didn't take the vows, so he wasn't able to complete his education. My mother was very bright, and she also ran a restaurant, Lupita's. But she had no opportunities to realize her educational and occupational goals. So for both my parents, education was a privilege, not a right. In our immediate family I was the oldest of four siblings—and three of us have post-graduate degrees."

Leticia's path to becoming a biology professor was not a foregone conclusion. Challenged by racism in both the public and private schools she attended in northern California, she was counseled by one teacher to focus on her typing ability rather than her academic skills, because, the teacher told her, "you probably wouldn't do well anyway if you got into a prestigious college." Undaunted, Leticia initially thought about applying to Harvard. Why, Harvard? She had heard one of the characters on the TV show *The Brady Bunch* talk about applying there! Instead, though, Leticia found out that Stanford University was in the same league as Harvard, only closer, so she applied there and was accepted.

Leticia was certain she wanted a career in science, but like many educated Latinos with a social conscience, she was concerned that a career in research would not be giving back to the Latino community. A professor at Stanford suggested that a teaching career at the college level would indeed be a way Leticia could give back to students and still be involved in research. After earning her Ph.D. at the University of California, Berkeley, and becoming a board member of the Society for the Advancement of Chicanos, Latinos, and Native Americans in the Sciences (SACNAS), Leticia not only became a professor at San Francisco State University but helped to design an innovative program to get minorities involved in the sciences. Funded by the National Institutes of Health's Minority Biomedical Research Support Program, the San Francisco State program ensures that minority students can earn money for working in the biomedical labs where they also are receiving instruction.

Well aware of the economic pressures on minority students, Leticia understands how much it means to them to be able to have this opportunity to further their careers by working in the science field—and also get paid for it. She also is conscious of the example she provides to minorities, especially Latinas. "Realizing when I was in college that I had never met a professor who looked like me or came from my background became my guiding light," she says. "Now, at San Francisco State, 66 percent of the student body are students of color. I found a purpose for my life at this campus, and this is the way I help my community. I am a role model, and that is very important for me."

Bringing creative teaching methods to her tremendously popular classes, Leticia employs "discovery-based" learning, which involves students coming up with their own hypotheses so that they have the opportunity to discover something completely new. "I can see where people get stuck not understanding things, so I've created techniques to cater to different learning styles," Leticia told me. She hopes to inspire more minority students to dedicate themselves, as she has done so passionately, to a career in the sciences.

But this *malabarista* is also passionate about her *mami* role and family life. How does she balance it with her life as a *profesora?* For one thing, she doesn't try to do everything herself. She is lucky enough to have her mother's help; her kids are often driven to soccer practices and other activities by their *abuela*—which is fine with them. And her husband is also an involved domestic partner, responsible for a number of household chores. The bottom line is that Leticia's family is behind her, because they know how much she loves her work. "My top priority is my family, but I have to do my work well in order to have a spiritual center. If everything is well in my family, then I can do things well at work."

One thing that is so central to Leticia's sense of inner balance is that her family understands what her work means to her. "Even when my children were very young, they understood that I needed to go and do my research. An example of how flexible my kids are is something that happened just this morning. I forgot to make my son's lunch, and he told me, 'Don't worry, *mami,* I'm going to buy my hot lunch today.' They are very supportive of my work, and that is so important to me."

In addition to being fortunate in having a supportive family, Leticia credits her ability to maintain a *malabarista's* balanced life to a very simple tool: to-do lists. Like María Elena Salinas, Leticia admits to being exceedingly organized. She told me that she loves to write down her to-do lists so she won't forget anything that needs her attention. And then she takes pleasure in crossing things off her lists. It seems that many women tend to have this amazing ability to prioritize and organize their time, even when faced with extremely busy lives. Leticia pointed to an interesting reason why some women are better at it than others. "Crossing things off my list—things that I've completed—motivates me to keep going. I cross, cross, cross, and I get it done. I recently read in a science magazine that the women who are the most productive in science—who write grants, do research, give presentations—are the ones who have families. And the reason is because we *have to* learn how to organize our time. If we have only a half an hour to do something, it's done in half an hour."

It's not all about lists, though. Leticia also talked about why she and a Latina colleague of hers seem to be able to handle certain stresses of an academic life when some others cannot. When faced with frantic deadlines and dueling responsibilities, she says that she and her friend are somehow able to acknowledge their feelings and think in terms of resolutions, rather than dwelling on their frustration. And that ability is key to maintaining a sense of inner balance.

An inspiration to her family, students, and colleagues, Professor Márquez-Magaña is a *malabarista* who delights in her roles as mother, wife, molecular biologist, and professor—and in the ability to invite all students into her exciting world of science.

If We're Such Talented *Malabaristas,* Why Do We Still Feel Guilty?

When I first came to the United States from Argentina with my daughter, Eleonora, I was already divorced. She was four years old at the time, and I was the sole provider for her, as I couldn't count on child support. So I worked and I went to school, because the psychology degree I had from Argentina wasn't sufficient to allow me to practice as a psychologist in the States. While I was studying for my Ph.D., I worked during the day, and at night and on weekends I went to school as well as taught Lamaze classes at a health center. This meant that I had to make arrangements for Eleonora. Some days my sister would take care of her, but other days I would take her with me to work or to school. She would take her coloring books and stay with me, often falling asleep on my lap. During the Lamaze classes, she was my assistant, helping me demonstrate how to hold the mother's legs when the baby is ready to be born, how to do the different breathing techniques, and a number of other things. It was fun! But I always questioned myself: "How is this going to affect my daughter? What will she say when she's an adult about being dragged to her mom's classes, having to help out as my assistant, and being so sleepy at the end of the night that she fell asleep in my lap instead of in her bed at home?" Feeling many of the same insecurities that all mothers have, I worried about the impact these memories—and my career—would have on her.

Unfortunately, many women are vulnerable to such feelings of guilt, about having a job or devoting themselves to a career at the same time that they're bringing up their children. Since Latinas often are taught that their role as a mother is supremely important, and is, in fact, the only career they should pursue, doing anything else makes them feel guilty. "Shouldn't my full attention be focused on my children?" they worry. And such guilt and worry can't help but undermine their sense of inner balance.

But we never should feel guilty for supporting our families or for pursuing a career that gives us a sense of self-worth and fulfillment. In our current economic climate, most of us have to work, but even those of us who don't should have the freedom to balance family and motherhood with personal achievement if we choose to do so. Child-care options are not as ideal as we need them to be, which is why many of us lend our support to the appropriate child-care legislation and make our voices heard. But children can flourish in a good child-care setting, and having your child spend part of his or her day in one doesn't mean you are not doing your job as a mom.

As for the persistent worry and guilty feelings? Let me bring you up to date on my daughter, Eleonora, as a way to convince you to put an end to any self-condemning thoughts. Several years ago, at the age of twenty-five, Eleonora got her Ph.D. in molecular biology from the University of Southern California. She loves her career as a bioinformaticist. She's also married to a great guy named Brian, is the mother of my darling two-year-old granddaughter, Sophia, and has learned from my example how to balance the joys of motherhood with the joys of a satisfying career. She wanted me to include the following statement about balancing work and parenthood—and not feeling guilty!

"I always thought that going to the Lamaze classes with my mom was fun. I never realized that she took me because she *had* to; I thought it was because she *wanted* to. Not all moms took their kids to work, so I thought I was lucky. Growing up and thinking about my future—there were absolutely no boundaries in my mind.

"Having both a career and a child myself now, it's not easy. I'm happy that I'm doing it, but I don't know how others do it alone. I have my husband to share the work at home, but if you're a working single mom, you really need somebody to help out. Even with my husband's help, I have very little time for myself at the moment. I'm learning to make more time, though. I recently bought a book to read for the first time in I don't know how long!

"As for feeling guilty? I don't feel at all guilty for having a career. I love my work and I love being a mom, and I wouldn't want to give up either one. And I think I'm a good role model, showing my daughter that if it makes you happy, you should have a career. I have friends who send their kids to day care and feel guilty about it, but I don't. My daughter learns things at day care—where she gets to relate to other kids and have stimulating activities—that she wouldn't learn if she were at home with me all day. I think some people feel guilty because they have a husband or a mother who thinks they should stay home full-time. I don't have anybody telling me that. I think the guilt often comes from people telling you what you should be doing. But if you feel comfortable with the situation, you shouldn't feel guilty. There have been people who asked me, 'Why did you want to have a child if you're not planning on staying at home full-time?' and I've always answered them, 'Why haven't you asked my husband the same question—or do you just ask the women?' "

I am sure that when little Sophia grows up, if that question about staying home is still being asked, she will have just as smart an answer as her mother.

Let Your Heart Set the Priorities:
Actress Elizabeth Peña

Given the multifaceted lives we lead, we're all familiar with the need to prioritize. Figuring out how to get it all done—or deciding *which* things to get done and which to postpone or let go of—can be an anxiety-producing assignment. To-do lists and day-planners are our constant companions, but it still comes down to some tricky decision making, often on a daily basis. Do I make a fantastic dinner for my husband and kids after work or pick up take-out and spend that extra hour helping my daughter with her math—or rewriting my résumé so I can apply for that exciting job I heard about? Prioritizing is all about "What is most important at this very moment?" and yet trying to answer that simple question throws some of us into a tailspin.

One very busy lady—gifted actress, director, mom, and wife Elizabeth Peña—has come up with her own proven methods of dealing with the twenty-first-century reality of being pulled in seventeen different directions at once. Star of Showtime's popular series *Resurrection Boulevard*, as well as numerous films, including *Tortilla Soup, Rush Hour, Down and Out in Beverly Hills,* and *La Bamba,* Elizabeth is the mother of a five-year-old daughter and a three-year-old son. She's also a caring wife and a daughter who is still very much involved in the lives of her parents. She divides her time between Los Angeles and the state of Washington, where she has homes; film locations; Miami, where her father lives; and New York, which her mother and sister call home. When I asked her if she sometimes doesn't feel like she lives on an airplane, she told me, "I live on the Planet Earth . . . but the plane is like a bus to me!"

Traveling is only one part of the balancing act featuring this talented and passionate mom-wife-daughter-actress, and Elizabeth wasn't always sure she could pull it off. She said that handling both an acting career and motherhood was a serious enough concern that she originally had planned to put off becoming a mom: "For years, I told myself—and I know many other actresses who have, too—I didn't want to have children until I'm successful, whatever that definition might be. My fear was, Oh, my God, if I have children, how am I going to be able to do my career, how am I going to be able to make money, how am I going to be able to choose projects I want and not do projects that I hate, just because I need to make money? But I've found that everything happens, everything settles in, the way it's supposed to. I took a year off with my first child, Fiona, and it was the year that *Lone Star* came out. I didn't go to the premieres, I did no press, and everybody was going 'You're nuts!' and I'm going 'No, I've been doing this since I was eight years old. If taking a year off means that it's all going to go away, then I didn't do a very good job of establishing myself.' But I came back to work, and even though in this town it's 'out of sight, out of mind,' I had employers refamiliarize themselves with me, and, you know—Boom! You're back!"

Part of the reason everything has settled in the way it's supposed to now that she's a working mom, said Elizabeth, is that her husband is available to be a stay-at-home dad when needed. An independent contractor, he is able to work his hours around Elizabeth's so that one or the other is always there for their young children. And spending lots of time with her kids is a must for Elizabeth, so she makes sure to arrange her schedule around them as much as possible. She says that she is never away from her kids for more than three days—"more than that is way too much"—and that if she knows she's going to be gone longer, they come with her: "I make sure that if I'm working, it's scheduled around my kids' activities. If there's a 'mom's day' at their school, I call and beg production to let me go. And the people at *Resurrection Boulevard* have so far been fantastic to me. So that helps a lot. And I have a great husband!"

Like the other *malabaristas* in this chapter, Elizabeth also defines herself as "a very good organizer." She writes down everybody's schedule, coordinates with her husband, and uses the same principle as a housewife and mom that she employs as an actress: When you're organized, you take the guesswork out of whatever you have to do: "If you do all your 'homework' on a film, then once you arrive at work, you can just fly, be free, you know? And the same goes for getting kids ready in the morning. My mother was extraordinarily organized. I remember as a child, the night before school she'd take out my clothes, fold them, have everything neatly stacked, so that you'd get up in the morning and everything's ready to go. I actually do that for my kids too, and my husband says it's so over-the-top. But, believe it or not, that saves me fifteen minutes in the morning, and when you start adding up fifteen minutes throughout your day, you end up acquiring an additional hour to do stuff you need to do — because inevitably, even if I'm working, I still have to go food shopping, make sure my babysitter is happy, that the cars are working, that the bills are paid, you know?"

Don't we all identify with Elizabeth's need to acquire just one extra hour in the day? One of the ways we can do this is to remember another principle that's so important in the business world and can be used in our homes as well: *Delega!* Give over some of your responsibilities to others so that we're not left doing absolutely everything ourselves. As we talked further, Elizabeth told me that her husband has been trying to convince her to get an assistant so that she can free up more of her time to spend with her children. Like many of us, though, Elizabeth was having reservations about delegating. Perhaps you'll relate to her argument? She said, "I come home sometimes and I have like thirty-two phone calls to return. And I hate the phone, because I want to get home and I don't want to communicate with anyone except my husband and my children. But when my husband asks me why I don't get an assistant, I think, 'You know why? Because if I get an assistant, it's going to take me triple the amount of time to explain what I need done when I can just go and do it in five minutes.' "

Sometimes we are so good at all the things we do, so well organized, and so used to doing it all that, like Elizabeth, we resist the idea of delegating some of our work. What I told Elizabeth was that maybe she should heed her husband's advice. It's true that training and orienting an assistant—whether it's an office assistant, babysitter, or housekeeper—takes time. But once they get to know you and understand just how you think and how you feel, what is important to you, and how you want them to do their job, they will free you from responsibilities that eat away at your time. And you will own more of it— to spend on the activities and with the people who really matter the most to you.

What matters most to Elizabeth is her "heart connection" to her work and the people she loves. In making decisions large and small— from major career moves to whether or not to attend "mom's day" at her child's school—Elizabeth follows her heart. She told me that her initial decision to become an actress was based on an experience that so touched her, her heart had made up her mind already: "When I was eight years old, I went to see a play, and I remember sitting on the aisle seat, halfway up the theater, riveted by the play. After the intermission, as the second act began, I moved up to a seat closer to the stage, because it was empty and I wanted to get as close as I possibly could. I can't even tell you the name of the play; all I remember was that the actress in it, her performance, at least from an eight-year-old's point of view, was so extraordinary that I literally, and this is going to sound ridiculous, I felt like I levitated off of my seat. And I was so blown away by it that when the play ended I ran crying to my mother, saying, 'That's what I want to do! I want to be an actress!' "

Like Elizabeth, once we have experienced a passionate connection to whatever it is we are involved in, or want to be involved in, we know that is where our heart lies. And making sure that you fill your day with enough things that give you that heart connection is what will result in a sense of inner balance. When I asked her what advice she might give to other Latinas who are trying to prioritize and make decisions that will give them this kind of spiritual equilibrium, Elizabeth had this to say: "I don't practice any particular religion, but I do believe that there is a great force that connects us all. And I think that if you feel like confusion is setting in, or that you're not happy for some reason and you can't put your finger on it, if you just stay quiet and listen for messages, listen to your inner heart, you can never go wrong. You can never make a bad decision."

Listen to what your heart has to say, and then set up priorities. It sounds almost too simple, but it works. Following your heart will guide you in such a way that you'll spend more time on what brings you the most happiness and fulfillment and less time on what matters least.

A Busy *Malabarista*'s Inner Resources
Actress Silvia Pinal

Don't we all marvel at how certain women, like the ones we've been hearing from in this chapter, manage to do all the things on a typical working mother's agenda—plus four or five or ten additional worthwhile activities? Perhaps you are one of these extraordinary women but can't quite put your finger on how you accomplish all that you do. Sometimes we have secrets for balancing our own busy lives that we're not fully aware of until we stop to think about just what gets us through our hectic days. I was thrilled to be able to speak with one of Mexico's living legends, actress Silvia Pinal, and to get the chance to ask her about her own *"malabarista* secrets."

A film actress since 1948, when she starred in *Bamba* with the pioneer director Miguel Contreras Torres, Silvia has acted in more than eighty-five films (including three by acclaimed director Luis Buñuel), won three best actress *Arieles* (similar to the Oscar in the United States), appeared in numerous television shows and musical theater productions, raised a family of three children, and been elected to both local and national office in Mexico. In addition to the many Mexican films she has starred in (including one she had just completed at the time of this interview, *Ya No Los Hacen Como Antes (They Don't Make Them Like They Used To)*, Silvia also enjoyed a film career in Spain and Argentina. Having read that she worked eighteen hours a day when she was a congresswoman, I asked Silvia what her secret was. How did she remain so energized? In our conversation she reiterated two themes that our other *malabaristas* also have mentioned: being organized and loving what you do.

"I learned when I was very young how to be organized," she told me. "I got married very young and also got pregnant at an early age, but I still worked as an actress, so I figured out a system to organize my house, take care of my children, and make an income so I could live a little better. I respect women who choose to stay home with their children all the time—God bless them—but when you love your children as well as something that you love doing, you learn how not to neglect either one. I love acting, I love musical theater, I love television—and in politics it is a delight to have the power and to use it well, to fight to get things done that I think are right. The pleasure and the interest that I have in doing these things that I enjoy, that's what gives me the energy."

When she was a congresswoman, Silvia was on a special commission that dealt with gender and women's issues. And today she hosts a television program entitled *Mujer, Casos de la Vida Real (Women's Cases from Real Life)*, on which women's problems are addressed. But how does Silvia deal with her own problems, including the need for quality time with herself? Each of us needs time to ourselves, to refresh and relax and center ourselves emotionally before returning to our work and to our families; without it we aren't much good to anyone, right? I wondered how Silvia could possibly fit this important "alone time" into her busy schedule. She said that she maintains a spiritual life by making use of that time when she's alone: "That's the time to think about myself, my problems, my life, my children, my work, or whatever is going on around me. There is not that much of it, but I use that time to the maximum. I use it to have a kind of spiritual adjustment."

When you know how to connect with that part of yourself that reflects your life from a spiritual perspective, you can bring your busy existence into balance. When you draw on this inner resource to assess what your life is all about and what is most meaningful for you, you can make the necessary adjustments to achieve a sense of peace and stability.

In Latin America there is a saying that *la soledad es mala consejera* (loneliness is a bad adviser). And yet spending time alone can be just what we need to clear our minds and refresh our spirits. What Silvia was saying about taking as much time as possible to be by herself—it's important. You can become your own best adviser if you take the time to be with yourself and listen to what you're feeling and thinking. Every day, when we wake up or when we go to sleep, or at another time during the day, we can nurture our relationship with ourself. At the end of the day, for example, we can take at least ten minutes to think about what we've learned from our day, what we did well, and what we could have done. This time alone can become a kind of ten-minute retreat to center yourself and consider what you really want from life.

Comedienne Liz Torres's Take on *Malabaristas*

Sometimes the most insightful wisdom can be found where we least expect it—in a joke, a cartoon, a funny scene in a movie. Those who have the gift of comedy teach us about who we are by making us laugh at ourselves. It is the laughter of self-recognition, because although comedy is an exaggeration of the way things are, we see ourselves in that overstatement and can't help but chuckle at the ridiculousness of the truth.

Our Latina treasure, actress and comedienne Liz Torres, is someone who never fails to reveal the absurd and hilarious truth in her comedic sketches. She has made us laugh on *The John Larroquette Show*, *First Monday*, *American Family*, *Gilmore Girls*, and in many other television shows, films, and theatrical performances. As she and I laughed our way through a conversation about how Latinas are such natural *malabaristas*, balancing all that we have to do and taking it all in stride, Liz spun out several humorous yet revealing scenarios, which I want to share with you now:

> I was watching *Oprah* and it was a show about women "taking time for themselves," taking care of themselves so they can have more of themselves to give. And Dr. What's-his-name said, "If you don't take care of yourself, you're cheating your children." Taking care of our selves? That's a foreign concept to Latinas! You know, there could be four men in a family, a father and three sons, and they're playing cards at the table—and the woman has just come home from the hospital after having a heart transplant, but still she's at the stove making tortillas with an "I.V." hooked up to her arm on one of those rolling things. And at the same time she's pushing around a vacuum, you know? There is no concept of "taking care of yourself" for a woman in a Hispanic household! We manage everything until we fall down. Then we have an excuse; but until then, if you're healthy and you're ambulatory, there's no reason for you not to make those tortillas unless you're dying. And even on your deathbed, you can still use your hands to make the tortillas, you know?

Do you see a little bit of yourself—or perhaps your mom or grandmother—in Liz's quasi-realistic fantasy? Isn't it true that Latinas have tended to overdo the balancing act by trying to accomplish everything ourselves while automatically letting the men in our lives off the hook? Have you ever stopped to think about how your family would survive if you went on strike? How about if all the Latinas in the United States went on strike? What would our men—and the rest of society—do then? Here's what Liz thinks might happen.

> I think the whole country would close down. Our men would have to come home and take care of our kids. And that would mean that the whole country would come to a complete standstill. There would be no manicured lawns, because there would be no gardeners—so the grass would grow so high that the country would turn into an absolute jungle. Everyone would be starving because there would be nobody out in the fields picking the food to eat. No one could go out to eat because there would be no cooks, waiters, or busboys. Anglo women would have to quit their jobs to come home and take care of their children, because we wouldn't be there to do it for them. The wheels that keep this country going would grind to a screeching halt, because all the jobs that the Hispanics do in this country—the ones that nobody else wants to do—would simply not get done. No factories, nothing! And worst of all—there'd be nothing to wear. There would be all these designers with fabulous drawings of clothes, but no workers to make them. And where would we be without fashion?

It's important to appreciate all that we do to keep our families, our communities, and our country functioning smoothly—and Liz definitely paints an out-of-control picture of life without us. But it's just as important to remember that we can't do it all, and that, as absurd as it might seem to traditional Latino families, Latinas in fact *do* need time for themselves!

Out of Balance/Balancing Too Much at Once

In order to maintain our centeredness, our inner balance, it's important that we give attention to the areas of our lives that make us whole. For many of us, meaningful work, children and family, and a loving relationship with a mate form the core of our daily existence. Being politically or socially active, engaging in religious or spiritual practices, and pursuing hobbies that challenge us and bring us pleasure are also part of who we are. But when we try to spread ourselves too thin on the one hand, or neglect aspects of ourselves that are important to us on the other, we lose our sense of well-being and balance. Here are the signs that you may be jeopardizing your *malabarista*'s equilibrium.

- If you are feeling depressed or out of sorts, you may be neglecting a part of yourself that's crucial to enjoying who you truly are. If you're spending way too much time at work and haven't had the chance to really hang out with your husband or your children lately, chances are you need to ease up at work and give yourself the time you deserve with your family. On the other hand, if you've been giving every waking moment to your work and your family—and haven't left any for yourself and the things you enjoy on your own, you're tipping the scales into that dangerous oversacrificing zone. Be as considerate of yourself as you are of others and become sensitive to what your out-of-balance feeling might signify.
- If you're feeling frazzled and overwhelmed much of the time, you're probably trying to do too much. And you're not alone. Many women, especially Latinas, feel that they have to be all things to all people—their children, husbands, friends, parents—in addition to being productive at work, exercising to keep in shape, and keeping a house that looks presentable. Scores of magazine articles and books are written to help us combat the Superwoman syndrome of feeling like we've got to do it all. I think the most important thing to consider once you've realized that you're trying to balance too many activities at once is this: What is most important right now—and what will make you feel better? Is it more important that your house is perfectly clean or that your children get a

bedtime story read to them? Will you feel better taking a bubble bath or answering all your e-mail? Slow down. Delegate to others in your household, including your children, some of those responsibilities that are making you crazy. In addition to helping you out, they'll be helping themselves by learning to take responsibility for their own needs and those of the family as a whole. And never forget about your own needs. You can't make anyone else happy unless you are relaxed and happy yourself. Reward yourself for all that you do by giving yourself the time to do what you love.

The *Malabarista*'s Practice: Bringing Your Day Into Balance

As a way to end this chapter on a balanced note, here are some simple strategies for bringing more balance into your day-to-day life. These ideas revolve around time, and figuring out ways to have more of it so that you can spend it doing what is most important to you.

Curandera Elena Avila says that the Aztec people actually came up with a mathematical formula for balancing human, family, community, and spiritual life based on the proportions of 52 percent, 26 percent, 13 percent, and 9 percent, which add up to 100 percent. The following advice may not be mathematical, but it stems from a similar spiritual goal: to bring our lives into balance so that we can feel more at one with ourselves, those we love, and the world to which we belong.

1. *At the end of the day write down all the things you have to do tomorrow.*
   Even when the list is long, it's less overwhelming when you've written down all your to-dos than when they're floating around in your mind and keeping you up at night.
2. *Go through the list and mark only the things that you must do tomorrow. Move everything else to a separate list called "pending."*
   For example, tomorrow you must pick up your suit from the cleaners because you need it for work the day after tomorrow. And you must take your daughter to the dentist. And you must make time to take a walk by yourself for a half hour—to ensure your health and peace of mind. How-

ever, you can postpone shopping for your son's school supplies and buying your friend's birthday gift until Saturday.

3. *Review your list and decide if some of these responsibilities are someone else's.*

    Maybe your teenage son or daughter is the one who should be picking up their shoes from the shoe repair. And maybe it's your husband's turn to do the grocery shopping. Be sure to delegate whenever it seems logical.

4. *Coordinate your agenda with your partner's.*

    Avoid having the two of you doing the same errands by checking in with each other on who's planning to do what. Is your husband planning to stop off at the drugstore after work today to pick up his prescription? If so, he could also pick up the items you need there so you don't both have to go to the drugstore on the same day.

5. *Do the little things first.*

    If your list seems endless and you can't seem to shorten it or delegate enough, tackle the little things that won't take very long first. For example, call your doctor to make an appointment, write a quick thank you note to your aunt. Once you take care of these easy-to-do chores, your list will shrink and you'll enjoy a feeling of relief.

6. *Make appointments to follow up later.*

    If calling back friends, family, or others is on your list, but you don't really have time to talk to them now, call them and tell them you are overwhelmed with the amount of work you have to do, but let them know that you remember them, want to speak with them, and will call them back later when you have more time.

7. *Always begin and end your day with an activity that revitalizes and relaxes you.*

    Choose something that you enjoy, something that restores you or comes from your heart. For example, riding your bike before the traffic is heavy, having a cup of tea by your favorite window, doing yoga, or listening to your favorite music. If you're feeling overwhelmed, even ten minutes of time for yourself at the beginning of the day—to think about yourself, your life, what you want, how you're feeling, your family, your loved ones—will give you the courage and energy and motivation to have a good day. At the end of the day, take time to release yourself from the tension, worry, and arguments that may have come up in the last twelve hours. Give yourself time to create peacefulness so that you will have a relaxing evening and a restful sleep. Being at peace with yourself and with the ones you love is at the heart of maintaining inner balance and enjoying a better quality of life.

8

La Reina's Confidence
and Strength

I have always had a very strong personality, but at the same time I
was always very shy — so I had to fight my shyness. I had a lot of con-
frontations with my mother, always, and I also had to confront situations that I felt were unfair, as in the fascist school I attended. I ended
up doing what I wanted to do, but with many difficulties. Nothing
was easy, especially when I started out in the theater.
— Norma Aleandro, actress

Although many accomplished women have worked hard to reach the
pinnacle of their professions, there are still those who believe that Latinas do not belong in such powerful roles outside the home. The old-
fashioned notion that women in general, and Latinas in particular,
are not really up to the task of succeeding in "a man's world" is often
held by those we are closest to, such as our fathers, husbands, or
boyfriends. On the other hand, every Latino man acknowledges the
lofty status his mother has within the family; in fact, he honors his
mother, sometimes to the point of viewing her as the embodiment of
the Virgin Mary or the Virgen de Guadalupe. So we tend to be seen by
those who love us as strong, important, and worthy of respect — but
perhaps only in the context of the home.

A woman's sons and daughters look to her for wisdom, guidance,
and nurturing. The term *reina del hogar* signifies a powerful position
within the household, and the sense of prominence that goes along
with that role gives women an inner strength and confidence. But how

do we take that confidence and run with it — in the direction we choose for ourselves? How do we use our strength to strive for and realize our dreams?

We're going to explore how a Latina's feelings of self-worth, derived from the high value our culture places on her role within the home, can be shifted over to whatever role you choose in the outside world. Certainly we need to learn the necessary skills and gain experience in the field we're aiming to succeed in. But faith in oneself is also an important piece of the developmental process that Latina Power represents. By integrating our experiences of having been in charge on the domestic front — either as a mother, elder sibling, daughter, or *comadre* — we can build the confidence and strength we need to advance along our personal path.

The stories in this chapter attest to the fact that accomplished Latinas from all walks of life have leveraged their inherited cultural status as "queen of the home" to become *reinas* in their chosen fields. They prove that it is well within our power to feel perfectly at home with our achievements and successes.

"Music Transports Me to Another Realm"
Opera Singer Eva de la O

Even when our family gives us the moral support to pursue our goals, society's values can still intrude, thwarting our plans and undermining our dreams. The belief that women ought simply to be good housewives and good mothers has been and still is held in cultures throughout the world, including many segments of Latino cultures. Opera singer Eva de la O confronted this entrenched belief throughout her life, but succeeded in spite of it. Her personal history also is filled with instances of family members being forced to adapt to society's constraints, but like others in her family, Eva found a way to follow her own course.

Born in Puerto Rico, Eva was exposed to the joys of music even as a young child. Her father was an excellent musician and played the *bombardino*, a brass instrument similar to a French horn. Eva's mother, an elementary school teacher by profession, was trained in piano and had a lovely singing voice. Although they had a good life in Puerto Rico, Eva's family moved to the United States when she was three for reasons that had little to do with economics. Her father had been divorced prior to marrying her mother, and marrying a divorced man was simply not acceptable in Puerto Rico. Since such mores of the time clashed with their own, Eva's parents' move to the United States represented an escape from the restrictions of a culture they otherwise loved.

In New York there were obstacles of a different sort. Although she had years of teaching experience and spoke perfect English, Eva's mother was unable to get a position as a teacher due to her "unacceptable" accent. So she took a job as a factory worker, something she had never dreamed of doing in Puerto Rico. Eva's father initially had a job digging ditches but later went to work as an accountant for the city government. The family thus paid their dues, but her parents' concern for Eva's education never abated. It always was assumed that Eva would go on to a music conservatory.

And she did. Attending the Juilliard School of Music in Manhattan, the most prestigious music school in the United States, Eva continued sowing the seeds for her musical career. But her neighborhood environment also played a significant role in her artistic growth. In the Latino barrio where she lived with her family in New York, there were rich and diverse cultural influences that nurtured the young singer creatively and intellectually. She felt part of a community of artists in classical music, none of whom were very well known at the time. Eva was determined to alter that. "I wanted to change the image of Latino musicians," she said. "People usually expect us to show up with a conga drum between our legs. They don't believe that we can play classical music. So in 1979 I formed a chamber music group called Música de Cámara to call attention to Puerto Rican musicians. I wanted to include artists of varying ages, because I have always had a strong belief that classical music does not end when you turn thirty-five years old, as some managers seem to think. We look at the quality of the artists and how a particular musician will enhance the group."

Unlike many other young Puerto Rican women at the time, Eva was not brought up to be a housewife. Her parents consciously raised her to be a musician, and she was lucky to have had such nurturing of her creative abilities. Going after the education she needed to pursue her dream of singing classical music would have impressed Eva's grandmother. After the American victory in the Spanish-American War the schools in Puerto Rico became coed and her grandmother was therefore prohibited from attending school, due to her father's concern about her being in a classroom with boys. Still, Eva's grandmother's desire to learn motivated her to educate herself. Because education, training, and music were valued so deeply by Eva's grandmother and parents, Eva never considered abandoning her education or career in order to be a *reina del hogar*. However, the realities of being a working mother presented unforeseen challenges.

For periods of time during her first marriage, Eva had to neglect her singing career in order to take care of her children and attend to the needs of her husband. She tried juggling her responsibilities and bringing her children with her to the theater when she didn't have a babysitter, but it became very stressful for her. Her husband also resented the time she spent on her career and, despite her efforts to put her family ahead of her life as a performer, their marriage ended in divorce. Discouraged and unhappy, Eva continued to try everything she could in order to stay connected to her life as a singer, but like so many women trying to balance family and career, she found herself having to put some of her aspirations on hold while she took care of her young children.

Despite her personal struggles, she received glowing reviews for her vocal performances and was encouraged by the close attention paid to her by key critics. J. Schulman of *Backstage* described her performance in the opera *Nabucco* by Verdi as "a voice that seems incredible . . . like something that has come out of the golden times of the opera." When she sang in Puerto Rico in *L'Enfant Prodigue* by Debussy, the critic from *Nuevo Día,* Sylvia Lamoutte, pronounced her "a total revelation . . . her pianissimos were delicate and emotional." Eva also distinguished herself by choosing a repertoire of Latin American composers, including Carlos Chávez, Hector Villa-Lobos, and Alberto Ginastera, who encouraged her greatly.

A second marriage brought problems similar to those in the first. Eva's husband could not accept her success, and the more her career flourished the more he felt threatened and began to distance himself from her. After her second marriage broke up, Eva feared she would not be able to stand on her own without a man in her life. However, she received much emotional support from her friends, especially from Siri Rico, another opera singer, her mother, and a psychologist friend from Puerto Rico, with whom she had many phone conversations. Eva also went into therapy to help overcome her fears of being a woman by herself. And ultimately she did.

Like many successful women, Eva de la O went through a lot of pain trying to accommodate men who essentially didn't understand her artistic goals or approve of her life. She told me that in both marriages she came to realize *"mejor sola que mal acompañada."* Although she values family and marriage, there was no way she could abandon her life as a musician, and therefore she had to make the difficult decisions to separate from men who could not accept her for who she was.

Music is Eva's mission in life, and she was unwilling to give it up in order to please a man. Having been on the brink of losing that essential piece of herself, she values all the more what it means to her now. Celebrated not only for her artistry as a singer but for founding New York's Música de Cámara, which began as a forum for Puerto Rican singers and instrumentalists but now features musicians and composers from throughout North and South America and the rest of the world, Eva is queen in a domain she'll never forsake. "Music transports me to another realm," she says. "It's a healer; it's nurturing. It lets me dream and go to unknown worlds, where there is no horizontal line between earth and sky. Everything is one."

"I Had the Burning Drive to Better My Life":
Recruitment Executive Fern Espino

Although our culture bestows the *reina del hogar* title on us—along with the expectations that go along with it—we must struggle to develop our queenly strength and competence in realms outside the home. And it's important to acknowledge that the effort we put into realizing our goals is not just the means to an end; the struggle itself is its own reward in that it strengthens us, builds our confidence, and solidifies our sense of who we are and what we're striving for. For some of us, our efforts to realize our dreams are met with negativity or resistance on the part of those who are closest to us. When this is the case, our most difficult struggles are often within our own family, and those difficulties frequently are based on deep-rooted values embedded in Latino culture. Fern Espino's story is an example of this kind of culturally-based family rift.

Recognized by *Hispanic Business* magazine as one of the Top 100 Influential Hispanics in America, former dean of student development at General Motors Institute (now Kettering University), charter member of President George Bush's Commission for Minority Business Development, and CEO of her own executive recruitment firm, Spanusa, Fern Espino is certainly a *reina* in her field—or should I say fields—but she didn't come by her distinguished career easily. She was brought up in Tucson, Arizona, in a Mexican family whose traditional beliefs about a Latina's role in society conflicted starkly with Fern's plans for her future, which included a college education and a good career. Her parents would tell her, "What makes you believe that you are better than us and everybody else?" Her mother never worked outside of their home, and her father was a laborer. They were always in debt—no assets, just paycheck to paycheck. "I had the burning drive to better my life," Fern told me, "so I made sure that I got an education, even though in doing so I was going against what my parents wanted."

Fern's mother would impress upon her, "If we don't have it, you shouldn't either. God wants you to be *humilde.*" And Fern also received strong messages—from her parents and other family members—that money is not important, that God will provide, that money is the root of all evil. "I also got the message that I was not supposed to make more money than my family," Fern recalled.

After receiving her Ph.D. from the University of Arizona and conducting postdoctoral studies at Harvard's John F. Kennedy School of Government and its Institute of Educational Management, Fern began her career in Texas at the College of the Mainland, where she was dean of college and financial services. During this time the U.S. Bureau of International Communication sought her consulting services on higher education programs in Africa, Mexico, and Switzerland. Fern was on a roll, but the disapproving messages she had received from her family continued to reverberate: "When I got to the point where I was making good money, I unconsciously began to sabotage my success. Because I always heard the voices of my parents, about not embarrassing them by having a career and doing things that a Mexican woman shouldn't be doing. Even though I had been on my own for years, I still heard my parents saying these things."

Like Fern, many Latinas can't shake the feeling that they're betraying their families when they become breadwinners or when they earn more money than their parents or husbands. Making more money than what you need to survive also brings up ethical conflicts, since it forces us to confront certain attitudes about money that are prevalent in Latino culture. For example: "making too much money is immoral"; "money corrupts"; "money goes to people's heads"; "it's wrong to earn too much money because it makes others envy you"; "women who make money become materialistic and forget about their families"; and, of course, "it's wrong to make more money than your husband."

Some of these attitudes can be traced historically to the time of the Spanish *conquistadores*, who were able to control the indigenous populations by teaching that God wanted people to be humble and unpretentious. And such teachings are ingrained in the Latino community to such a degree that many never question their validity.

One person who has questioned these ideas is Lionel Sosa, in his important book *The Americano Dream: How Latinos Can Achieve Success in Business and in Life*. He points out that the Catholic Church often transmits contradictory messages, depending on the congregation being addressed. The overall message of masses performed in English, he contends, is one of hope, while the message of masses performed in Spanish is the virtue in subservience. In other words, he says, the Church teaches Latinos, not Anglos, that it is virtuous to be poor, and that by suffering as a humble person throughout your life you assure yourself of being welcomed into Paradise.

As a matter of fact, Fern also mentioned that what she had heard at home about the evils of money echoed what she heard at church. "The Church reinforced things my mom told me, like 'Don't think about money. As God gives to the birds and to Nature, He's also going to give to you.' They would give you the message that money was the way to evil, that you couldn't be rich and spiritual because those two things are not compatible."

If the Church, consciously or not, holds Latinos in the United States back from being as ambitious as their Anglo counterparts (this was Lionel Sosa's and Fern's experience, but probably not the case in all churches), we have to consider how that message is compounded with respect to Latinas, who are taught so often by their families to focus solely on becoming wives and mothers. Given the disincentive by both her church and her family to become a success, it is almost miraculous that Fern has accomplished all that she has in the worlds of business, education, and community leadership. And to what does this *reina* attribute her triumph over such negative, antiquated attitudes? A supportive *comadre* and a set of "blinders," which Fern used to block out any pessimistic or disapproving influences that might have inhibited her from reaching her goals.

"There was one woman who really helped me," Fern told me, "and that was in my undergraduate days. She was a secretary to the registrar, and she's the reason why I continued on after the bachelor's degree to get my Ph.D. under a grant. She told me I could do it and convinced me that once I had my education no one could take it away from me — I could do whatever I wanted to do. And as for what allowed me to overcome the negative messages I received, I didn't give myself an opportunity to look sideways. I just kept my blinders on and kept going forward. I set goals and wrote them down. When I went to college, I set ten-year goals and just persevered. I did what I needed to do."

Fern refused to allow anyone or anything to stand in the way of what she wanted to achieve. Although she once had been vulnerable to the unsupportive attitudes of family members and her church, she learned to honor her ambition — and to become a *reina* whose accomplishments and strength inspire others.

Women's Empowerment and the Catholic Church

Fern's experience of feeling disapproved of by her church for wanting to become a successful woman is not unique. Nor is the Catholic religion alone in historically having looked upon women as secondary to men. But since so many Latinas are adherents of the Catholic faith, it is important to consider some of the positive changes that have taken place in the Catholic Church in the last twenty years with respect to its treatment of women.

Until 1983, women were strictly forbidden to touch sacred objects such as the chalice or altar linen; they could not distribute holy communion, enter the sanctuary except for cleaning purposes, read sacred scripture from the pulpit, serve mass, or become full members of lay organizations. Due to the activism of the women's movement in the early 1970s, more equitable policies were developed within various religious institutions, including the Catholic Church. Girls may now be altar girls, and women may now read from the pulpit, lead prayer services, and distribute the holy sacrament, the most sacred aspect of the mass. Although the ban on ordination of women as priests remains, a growing number of Catholics, as well as organizations such as the Women's Ordination Conference (WOC), are working to lift it. The WOC also advocates "reclaiming the Church's early tradition of a discipleship of equals, promoting inclusive spiritualities which are liberating and feminist, and celebrating our diversity of gender, race, ethnicity, sexuality, language and symbol." They believe that decisions affecting the life of the Church should reflect female as well as male experience and thought.

When our religious institutions reflect a respect for women's equality and self-determination, fewer Latinas will have to go through the guilt and self-sabotage that Fern Espino overcame so valiantly.

Latinas and Money

Learning to become a *reina* in the workplace or the business world involves coming to terms with your outlook toward money. As Fern Espino's story points out, the first way we can do this is to consider the cultural beliefs about money that may have been handed down to us by our family or religious institutions. Once we become more aware of how restrictive ideas may have inhibited our aspirations, we can take steps to counter them. For example, we can learn to become more assertive when negotiating an appropriate salary or asking for a raise — and to feel that we're worth it.

But how do we develop that sense of inner confidence so that we really believe we're worthy? That process can begin with an acknowledgment of our Latina Power strengths. Consider the many important ways in which you are a *creativa, diplomática, aguantadora, atrevida, malabarista, comadre,* and *reina,* and how these valuable qualities contribute to the group or enterprise with which you're connected. Isn't that contribution worth the level of compensation you're asking for (or are already receiving but do not feel entitled to)?

Becoming more conscious of the many ways money can change our lives for the better helps to counteract the cultural bias against earning too much, which can hold us back. There is a popular saying in Spanish: *El dinero hace bailar al chango* (Money makes the monkey dance). Money can allow us to think, imagine, create, plan, and act, and we should not feel embarrassed or defensive about making it. Earning an income that provides more than the essentials frees us from the stress of living paycheck to paycheck that so many Latinas unfortunately experience. We should appreciate our earning capacity and recognize how our lives are enhanced by it. When we earn enough money to cover more than the bare necessities, we can use it to ensure our own and our family's welfare, to give ourselves and our children the opportunities for a superior education, to create political and social change in our communities and countries, and to fully enjoy our lives with the people we love.

An Important Fringe Benefit of Economic Independence

There is another way in which money—or, more specifically, a woman's financial independence—can change our lives. The connection might not seem obvious, but the link between a woman having her own income and the decreased likelihood of her being a victim of domestic violence is a strong one. This issue, which affects millions of Latinas throughout the world, was the subject of a recent report issued by the World Bank. The report features studies in Latin America showing that domestic violence is reduced as the participation of women in the labor force increases. One study in Nicaragua found that 41 percent of women who are not working for a salary are victims of severe domestic physical violence, while only 10 percent of those who are working for a salary outside the home suffer such violence. For example, women who work in a family business without an income are victims of domestic violence more frequently than those who earn a salary.

From a psychological perspective, these findings point to one of the cornerstones of the transition from *reina del hogar* to *reina* of your own destiny: self-esteem. Once you know that you can earn money, you feel differently about yourself. It's not just that you have money to support yourself, it's the feeling that you don't need to depend on anybody, the feeling that what you do is worth something to other people. Our society rewards worth with money, so once a woman starts working and sees her value in terms of financial compensation, she can't help but feel empowered. Once you sense that empowerment within yourself, you feel that other people owe you respect, that you can establish boundaries, that you can draw the line. It is when a woman is unable to draw that line that she allows herself to take abuse.

"The Feminist Movement Made an Impact on Me Forever"
TV Journalist Cristina Saralegui

Raised in a wealthy family in Cuba in the 1950s, as a child Cristina Saralegui assumed she would grow up to become an *ama de casa*, a housewife. But political and social upheaval, as well as her own personal transformation, resulted in a very different agenda for Cristina. Her path to becoming *reina de la televisión* began with her coming of age during the time when women in the United States were creating a culture-changing movement to expand their opportunities.

Cristina told me that everything changed for her when her family was forced to leave Cuba: "Exile was cruel, and everything that I learned in my native country was shrinking. We moved to Miami in 1960, and I attended university at the end of the 1960s. At that time the feminist movement made an impact on me forever." Even before she made the decision to go to the University of Miami to get her degree in mass communications and creative writing, Cristina had a strong sense of wanting to be an independent woman. As a teenager she realized the importance of working to earn her own money. "I have always been very independent, and as such I didn't want to be under the financial control of my father," she said. "I remember that when I was sixteen years old, I asked him for money. He took me to my closet, pointed to my clothes, and said, 'What do you want money for, with all of these clothes in your closet?' I didn't answer him, but the next day I left the house and looked for a real job, because I didn't want to have to tell him why I wanted money. There is no real independence without economic independence!"

Cristina's first job after graduating from the university was as an intern in the photo library at *Vanidades*, the number-one Latin American women's magazine, formerly owned by her grandfather. Since her formal education had been in English, it was a challenge for her to learn to write professionally in Spanish, but she did so winningly. After a number of other positions with Latin American magazines, Cristina became editor-in-chief of *Cosmopolitan en Español*, distributed throughout Latin America and the United States. During her stint at *Vanidades* she had met her first mentor, Elvira Mendoza, Colombian editor-in-chief of *Vanidades Continental* and a pillar in Latin American journalism, and at *Cosmo* she began a lifelong relationship with a second, Helen Gurley Brown, editor-in-chief of the United States *Cosmopolitan*, whom Cristina referred to as "majestic . . . and even today she continues to be my greatest mentor and professional *mamá*." Both of these women helped Cristina attain *reina* status in the journalism world.

After ten years at the helm of *Cosmo* Cristina resigned in order to launch what would become a Latina institution. She became executive producer and host of *El Show de Cristina*. Featuring star interviews as well as educational, issue-oriented topics such as teen pregnancy, AIDS, gay rights, child abuse, gangs, and breast cancer, the acclaimed show had a huge following and a successful run of twelve years.

After it ended in December 2001, Cristina began devoting her time to her weekly prime-time show on Univision, *Cristina: Edición Especial (Cristina: Special Edition)*.

There is a thread running through all of Cristina's media accomplishments, and that is her desire to learn and to teach. What continues to be important to her is the opportunity to reach out to the community and offer them—as well as herself—a chance to discover something important that they didn't already know. "I learn from everybody and everything—from the good as well as the bad," she says. "I am on a quest. I want to know what life is all about. The greatest challenge on my show is to educate and open the minds of my audience without offending them. Our people need information, and we try to teach them that they shouldn't be embarrassed to ask for help. Also, we try to teach people how to live together in this country without abandoning their Latin roots."

What Cristina hopes people learn from her shows is that we live in a world that is not perfect and that as such we are an imperfect species. "Even though we should always strive and aim for excellence," she says, "we must also learn how to accept change and shortcomings as a way to growth and learning. These are the biggest lessons I have learned from all those wonderful and diverse guests on my show, some courageous, some cowards, but all fascinating, imperfect humans trying to live their lives."

As *reina de la televisión*, Cristina has become one of the most powerful Latinas in the media. When I asked her where she draws her sense of inner strength and confidence from, she told me that it is a combination of things. Of course to be successful in one's career, she says, "you must work hard, get the training you need, create good relationships with other people, be loyal and honest, set the right goals for yourself, overcome your fears, and never give up. And you must create a purpose for your life, one that inspires you." But there is another element that contributes significantly to Cristina's power, and that is her spiritual life: "I was raised Catholic, but over the years I kept searching and enhancing my knowledge and faith, experimenting with metaphysics, transcendental meditation, and other spiritual practices. In terms of my material success, I appreciate being compensated for a job well done, but I also understand that we are much more than our material selves—and that our soul and spirit continue beyond this life."

I have appeared on several of Cristina's shows, and I must tell you that she is a very special person. A dynamic woman who sets high standards for herself and everyone who works on her team, she is deeply committed to the free exchange of ideas. She gave me an open platform to communicate my ideas without imposing herself, as some TV hosts do. Giving her guests and audiences the utmost respect, she created a home for Latinas where every issue relevant to our lives could be discussed intelligently and frankly. On my own talk shows and in my private practice I very often hear from patients and audience members, "Oh, I learned that on the *Show de Cristina!*" Cristina Saralegui has taught many women to stand up for themselves, to approach their lives with dignity, and to open up their minds to be able to dream of a better life. I salute her—and, like so many other Latinas, miss her daily show.

Reina in a Man's World
Linda Alvarado, President and CEO of
Alvarado Construction, and Owner of the Colorado Rockies
Major League Baseball Franchise

Wanting to get the real inside story about how a successful Latina navigates within an almost exclusively male world, I immediately thought of Linda Alvarado. *Reina* of *two* men's worlds—the construction business and professional baseball—Linda is indeed a breaker of barriers. Talking to Linda is an invigorating experience. She is so upbeat and so filled with enthusiasm for all the projects with which she's involved, one definitely gets the sense that this lady loves her life. The story of Linda's success began with the gifts bestowed upon her by her parents, not the material kind, but the intangible ones that build a person's confidence and sense of self. The only girl in a family with five sons, Linda never felt her parents wanted any less for her than they did for their boys. She talked glowingly about playing baseball and basketball with her brothers growing up, and about becoming a catcher as a little girl, because that was her dad's position on the team he played for.

But sports weren't all he and Linda's mom encouraged Linda to get involved in. "Certainly the cultural norm for Hispanic mothers when I was growing up was not to be encouraging your daughter to play sports, but to be more traditional, and to teach them to sew and cook and all those kinds of things," Linda told me. "But both my mother and father were always very encouraging and didn't treat me any differently than my brothers. They have a gift, because they are very positive people. They come from very, very humble economic backgrounds, but they enabled all of us to see the best in ourselves, even when we were not the best. And so this gift of self-confidence allowed us to do things. My parents were aware of the bias they had confronted, but they wanted their children to be educated and to be risk takers."

Becoming the owner of a construction company certainly qualifies as a risk for any woman, and particularly for a Latina. So how did this unconventional career choice come about? Linda confesses that although she and her brothers enjoyed building forts in their backyard when she was young, her professional path was actually the result of a fortuitous accident. "When I went to college I had a choice," she explained. "In order to earn money to supplement my academic scholarship, I was offered either work in the cafeteria or in the botanic gardens, which were in the process of being built. I thought, 'Okay, let me get this straight. I get to wear Levi's to work, I'll get a great tan, and I'll be working with all these fabulous men,' because I was single then, right? 'And I'll get paid to do this!' So I thought, 'Wow, this is cool!' And the botanic gardens job became my first work experience on a construction site."

Linda worked for the same construction company the following summer, gaining new skills and immersing herself in the nuts-and-bolts of the business. Being the savvy *reina* that she is, however, she didn't stop there. She realized she would need to bring something unique to her next employer if she wanted to shine, something that would set her apart from others trying to break into the field. "I really liked working on a construction site," she remembered. "So I went back and took classes in surveying, learned to read a blueprint, etc. But the most important class was one in computerized scheduling, which was revolutionizing the industry then. Our job-cost reporting systems are based on that. Taking that class enabled me to have a skill that most men didn't have, so I carved out a niche for myself in an industry that really did not welcome me."

What "not being welcomed" amounted to was nothing less than sexual harassment. For example, being the only woman on a construction site, Linda shared the outdoor toilet facilities with her male coworkers and often found degrading drawings and comments on the walls, "drawings of me in various stages of undress, with comments implying I didn't belong in this job." Discouraged by such treatment, the thought occurred to her that maybe she should just quit, but she loved the work and was determined to stick with it. When I asked her how she dealt with the harassment, I realized that even back then Linda's optimism and inner strength had helped her break through the roadblocks.

"My coworkers questioned my motives in ways that they would never question men," she said. "Their attitude was 'Why are you doing this? Who do you think you are?' But I just felt over time that I needed to deal with it with a little bit of humor—not that sexual harassment is funny—it definitely isn't. But I would find ways to say things like 'Well, gee, at least I look really good in a hard hat!' I'd make light of it to balance what really was a situation that was not positive. And certainly now it's against the law. But even within that environment, I really did like doing my job."

There were still times when Linda wondered why she was putting herself through such stress when she could have entered a field more openly accepting of women. Not only did her coworkers erect barriers she constantly had to knock down, but certain relatives questioned her goals as well. Again, it was Linda's parents who provided her with validation when such opposition arose. "My mother would try to explain to my relatives that I was a contractor, and they would respond, 'Well . . . why? What made her go into that kind of work?' But my mother always encouraged me to stay committed to my goals. She's four-feet-eleven, and she would simply tell me, 'Mijita, start small but think big!' So I started dreaming of building small projects, and my mother was a great advocate. She had never worked outside of the home, and was not experienced in business, but she really was a champion when it came to those situations where you ask yourself 'Why am I doing this?' Through all the difficult times, both she and my dad were a great support system."

Heeding her mom's advice, Linda began thinking big—and started small. Her first independent project was a series of bus-stop kiosks. Meanwhile, day by day, she knocked on doors, sometimes got rejected, but over time developed a track record, liquidity, and more confidence in her ability to build her own company. That *reina*'s confidence was not shaken even as she learned to sign her name "L. Alvarado" instead of "Linda Alvarado." She told me that if she had signed "Linda" prospective clients would know she was a woman, and she therefore wouldn't get the work. "I wasn't embarrassed about being a woman, but I realized I would be eliminated from consideration if they knew."

Over the long haul, though, how does a woman, a Latina, combat sexist and racist attitudes when she is working in a world given over primarily to Anglo men? Angry protest certainly won't allow you to follow through with your game plan of becoming a successful *reina* in your field. So how is it done? Linda has had plenty of experience dealing with this problem: "To confront those attitudes," she said, "you need balls, you need humor, and you need to focus on your goals despite other people's narrow vision of what you can accomplish. I think it's critical to have determination and to go a different route if the first one doesn't get you there. What I'm selling, first and foremost, is credibility—that a woman-owned, and Latina-owned construction company can build a project that is high quality, on time, on budget, the same as anyone else can. I don't want to be eliminated by the double whammy of negative stereotypes about women and Hispanics."

Linda said that women on construction sites have been viewed as secretaries, not owners. And Latinos on construction sites have been viewed as laborers, not the owners. So overcoming these views isn't easy, and very different every time. Attitude is as important as aptitude. At this point in her career her track record precedes her, but what she's trying to do is not only pursue her goals but change traditional thinking as well: "You can't change people overnight, so you need to continue to be diplomatic in your communication with them."

Humor, balls, focus, diplomacy—and knowing that you have the skills and talent to warrant your success—these strategies can diffuse potential conflict when you're the only woman or the only Latina in a potentially hostile or unwelcoming environment. But how do these tools actually play out in the context of a conference room or a work site? Linda's confidence in her ability to be a competent leader, as well as her belief in the importance of listening to and learning from those on her staff, enable her to maintain a relaxed, positive, professional outlook even though she is a Latina in charge of two enterprises largely dominated by men. But how might she handle a specific situation—for example, an off-color sexist or racist joke? "You don't want to be as off-the-wall about correcting people as they are about making an off-color joke," she responded. "I would change the direction of the conversation without correcting them and telling them they're wrong. Using humor to soften the edges a little bit, at my expense perhaps, but also getting them to refocus on those things that are important. Setting an example and changing the dynamic is important. I'm a fun person, I think I have a great sense of humor, I can laugh at myself, and I can laugh at situations, but not in a way that is demeaning to others."

Although Linda has had to forge a new path—there were no other women contractors when she was building her business—and has come up against negative stereotyping along the way, it is quite clear that she loves what she does and enjoys the people she works with. She told me that she's "very comfortable working in male environments—maybe because I grew up with brothers."

There was one other strategy, though, that Linda wanted to make sure to mention, as a way to break the ice when you're the lone woman in a world of men: "Sports! Men talk about sports, so being able to communicate by reading the sports page has been really important. Discussing not just serious business but small talk—that's something I learned early on. Who's doing what in the standings, who got traded—that's the universal language of men!"

Not only is Linda's company successful, and not only is she the first Hispanic owner of a major league baseball team, recipient of dozens of awards and honors—including the United States Hispanic Chambers of Commerce's Business Woman of the Year, the Revlon Business Woman of the Year, and one of *Hispanic Business* magazine's 100 Most Influential Hispanics in America—I think what is so beautiful about her story is that it embodies the values her parents instilled in her. They didn't just expect Linda and her brothers to do well in school and get good jobs. They also expected their children to contribute to the welfare of others—and to be leaders in the best sense of that word. "My mother and father were very adamant about encouraging us," Linda told me. "Whether it was in church, or in school, or in sports—you couldn't just be a member; you had to become a leader. Which meant you raised your hand to volunteer, or you raised your hand to assume responsibility. The interesting thing is that, as you do that, your self-esteem grows, because you feel like you are contributing.

You're someone who is interested not just in your own goals but in something that's larger than just you."

Guided By an Internal Light
Actress Norma Aleandro

Sometimes we assume that the supreme *reinas* of this world—the ones whom we admire most and even idolize a bit—were simply born with the strength of character that it takes to be outstanding in their field. But such strength rarely comes easily; on the contrary, it is developed throughout a lifetime, by repeatedly standing up to tough challenges and constantly tapping those inner resources that enable you to stick to your path, even when others might give up. Revered Argentine screenwriter, director, poet, and actress Norma Aleandro, star of *Son of the Bride, Autumn Sun,* the Academy Award–winning *The Official Story,* and many other films, exemplifies such depth of character. Born to parents who were actors, and cared for by her grandmother when her parents were on tour, Norma faced one of her greatest challenges when she was only nine years old. Her brave response to an occurrence of injustice was evidence of the moral strength Norma was capable of. And it changed her life.

Norma went to a school in Argentina run by Nazi sympathizers. During World War II, she remembers that they engaged in fundraising activities to send money to Germany. There were only a few Jewish students in the school, and three of them were in Norma's religion class. "The Jewish students were sent out of our class and told to go to the hallway where students were sent to be punished. There they were supposed to attend a special class on 'morals,' " Norma explained to me when we spoke. "I argued with the teacher, saying, 'Why shouldn't these students be given a book to study their own religion?' My protest became a scandal, but at that moment I decided that I would go to that same 'morals' class with my Jewish classmates. Everyone at the school was against me, but it was a way for me to make a statement about something that was unfair. I was nine then. By the time I was thirteen, I left that school because I couldn't take it anymore."

Promising her parents that she would study on her own, Norma never returned to that school nor attended any other. But she had an intense desire to learn and a love of reading. Although her family rarely had enough money to buy books, her grandmother, an insatiable reader herself, subscribed to a magazine called *Leoplan*, which published stories by such classic authors as Edgar Allan Poe and Guy de Maupassant. Norma credits that magazine with being very fundamental to her education. She also was drawn to anthropology, comparative religion, and Shakespeare—at a very young age. "Reading the tragedies of Shakespeare when I was nine I only understood about thirty percent of what I was reading. The rest I imagined."

Young Norma's education didn't end with reading and study. The environment in which she grew up also provided a "classroom" where she learned about diverse types of people, the theater, and life. "After I left school I was sent out into a much better world," she recalls. "On this other side I had a place in the theater, acting and living with actors, where there were none of those ethnic biases against Jewish people or any other group. It was a much more liberal world, a much richer life, accepting of the differences among people. Also, my uncles had a circus, and there were midgets, Gypsies, and others who didn't fit the norm. Everybody was treated the same way. So I had the good fortune of being educated with very good moral values, which gave me the opportunity to choose my path according to what my own sensitivity taught me, what I wanted for myself. I felt that this kind of society in the theater and in the circus was much more fair. I could be there without feeling as lonely as I had been in school."

But at the age of thirteen Norma faced yet another challenge— this time one that nearly cost her her life. Already convinced that she wanted to be an actress, she began studying with a French professor who was well known for bringing the Stanislavsky method of acting to

Buenos Aires. Considered a master by those in the acting community, this woman was Norma's role model — gifted, intelligent, cultivated, and elegant. Her arrival from France was met with much fanfare, and yet her interaction with Norma had devastating consequences. "In our very first class we were asked to demonstrate our skills to the professor," Norma recalls. "I went to the stage, and she asked me to do an improvisation. After I finished, she said to me, 'Do you want to be an actress?' And I said, 'Of course, I want to!' She told me, 'No. Don't continue. You're not good at this.' Being only thirteen, her criticism had a profound impact on me. I became suicidal. This was a woman whom I considered a genius, so whatever she had to say was fundamental to my thinking."

As a result of the acting professor's comments, Norma thought about suicide for a long time. She even stopped eating and became anorexic, although they didn't have a name for it in those days. She told me that "as I questioned whether I wanted to live or die, there was a very strange internal light that told me to keep going, to keep believing, to keep myself in life. I would go to church, not to mass, but to mediate, and it helped me to escape the noise of the world. It kept me in touch with the life that I love. I realized that what I *didn't* like was this professor's response to my wishes to be an actress. But I *did* love life."

One of the many lessons Norma took from this experience is that a person can be gifted at their craft and yet cruel as a teacher. Today Norma never neglects to tell acting students that they shouldn't allow themselves to be manipulated and should be cautious about overly critical or sadistic professors. Although Norma didn't return to that particular professor's class, she did not abandon her acting instruction. Her internal light propelled her onward to more classes, participation in numerous theater productions, and familiarization with a diverse theatrical repertoire.

Still, she came up against yet another serious obstacle to her career: intense stage fright. "I continued doing theater, but I always approached the stage with a panic that I wasn't good enough. And this stayed with me for many years. This wasn't just my professor's fault [for having been overly critical], it was within myself. I didn't yet have the technical preparation to allow me to create without difficulty. When I acquired those techniques, it allowed me to feel comfortable with the possibility of elaborating my character and to be able to touch the distinct 'melody' of the piece I am a part of."

Another life lesson derived from Norma's early professional experience: Authentic self-confidence is built on preparation. We can't talk ourselves into feeling strong and confident if we haven't adequately prepared for the project we're undertaking, whether it's a play, a board meeting, or a classroom of high school students. Once Norma had the technical preparation under her belt, she experienced that feeling of being comfortably in command. It was only then that she was able to be in touch with the essence—the melody—of the work she was engaged in. When we feel that closeness to the melody in our work we know we are on the brink of attaining *reina* status.

Although Norma told me that she believes *machismo* is a subtler problem in Argentina than in other Latin American countries, she had to grapple with its effects throughout her career, especially in the days when equitable treatment of women had yet to enter the consciousness of the culture. For an actress, the experience of sexual harassment— although not known by that label at the time—was commonplace. "I was working on a production and suddenly my contract wasn't renewed," she recalled, "and I didn't know why. And then a coworker said to me, 'Well, if you had said *yes* when so-and-so had asked you for certain favors . . . ' Probably it was just that this man had invited me to a meal or to go out or something, but I didn't want to have that kind of a relationship with that person, and it was hard for me to realize that my 'no' had a consequence. That experience made me much more aware, because that's when I started to detect certain ulterior motives in some of the powerful men with whom I worked."

Resourceful and determined, Norma used her new awareness of sexual harassment in the theater business as an impetus to create a more liberated working environment for actors like herself. As a young woman, she was instrumental in developing theatrical cooperatives, banding together with other actors, writers, and producers to launch their own productions. Not only did the women in these groups have more equality, all the participants had the opportunity to practice their art without waiting for the powers-that-be to give them work. Although today she is highly sought after as an actress, Norma continues to be a strong believer in taking theater to the streets, where its origins lie. And she counsels young actors to do just that: "Theater is the product of a social need that started with the shamans and the gathering of tribes, and then to the neighborhood street corners where people would meet. So as actors we can go back to those places. Even when you don't have money, you can still do theater. You can do it yourself; it's in your own hands."

This wonderful actress, who moved audiences with her exquisite performances as the outraged adoptive mother in *La Historia Oficial* and the lonely but reticent single woman in *Sol de Otoño* has seen tremendous changes in her field and in the world since her first appearance on the stage. In fact, she told me, actresses were originally considered "on the same level as prostitutes—which is why theaters are closed on Mondays, the day prostitutes had off. It was assumed that a woman in the theater was leading a loose life." While acknowledging that sexism still exists, Norma is very hopeful about the future of her profession. Her hopefulness rests on the improving prospects for female writers and directors.

"There are very few writers who have described women [accurately]," she told me. "Most plays written by men are the representation of a man's perspective. We are served by a masculine literature, a masculine philosophy, a form of intelligence that is masculine . . . But we have many more women writers today, in fiction and nonfiction, theater, poetry—and more film directors as well. When there are more female writers and directors, we will see ourselves reflected more clearly. It is already happening, and when women describe themselves, we not only hear about the problems of women, but it's also the way of expressing, of showing, using a vocabulary that is more feminine."

Norma Aleandro is *la reina del teatro* and film not only because her award-winning performances shine a penetrating light on the human spirit, but because she cares so deeply about her art, her fellow actors, and the world community of fellow human beings to which she feels genuinely connected. Like the little girl who refused to go along with the mistreatment of her Jewish classmates, the self-educated teenager who took pride in her uncles' circus of diverse artists, and the young woman who banded together with others to create a liberated theater cooperative, Norma continues to share her love and concern for humanity every opportunity she gets.

Overly Confident or Not Confident Enough

Being tremendously confident *es fabuloso*. The only way that *too much confidence* can hurt you is when you don't have the expertise, focus, and commitment to back it up. What do you want to be a *reina* of? Are you aware of the training and experience you'll need to become accomplished in your field and have you obtained those? Have you networked with your *comadres* to find out if the direction you're headed in is fraught with particular obstacles for which you'll need to prepare yourself? Authentic confidence means you know you're well prepared and therefore look forward to the challenge. An attitude of bravado or cockiness, on the other hand, can mean you might be fooling yourself about your actual qualifications. Remember, too, that educating and expanding yourself is an ongoing process. Regardless of how much you already know, how strong and confident you feel already, there is always something new to learn.

When we speak of *too little confidence* in the context of making the transition from *reina del hogar* to *reina* of whatever you choose, we're referring to a reticence to step out of the home environment and into the wide world outside it. If you are happy and comfortable being a stay-at-home wife or mom, that's fine. A homemaker's life can be a very fulfilling one, as many women will attest to. However, if the reason you are staying close to home is that you are fearful of having a connection to the outside world and need to be protected by the man in your life, you could be in trouble. This rationale means that you are giving over your power and your life to someone else. But we don't want to give that personal power away. We each own our own life and are responsible for it. So what are you waiting for? Look back at the previous strengths and think about how you can use them to develop your talents and interests. You don't have to depend on anyone else. You have yourself—and your untapped Latina Power!

Exercise: Visualizing the *Reina* You Will Become

One way that we become *reinas* is by integrating into our own being the experiences of the women we know or know about who represent confidence and strength. In trying to visualize yourself as "queen of the entrepreneurial world" or "queen of investigative journalism" or "queen of the biotechnology lab"—whatever realm best represents your aspirations—you can use your role models as a jumping off point for your own *reina* development. As *comadres* we are all here for each other, lending our support so that each of us becomes *reina* of the life we choose.

Now, here is the *Reina* Visualization Exercise, which can help you get in touch with your own power through the strength and inspiration of others.

Begin by closing your eyes and making sure that your body is in a comfortable position. Follow the flow of your breathing. Bring your body and your mind into balance.

Imagine now that you are on a beach, at the mountains, or in a forest—a place where you have been before or a new one that you would like to create. Feel yourself very comfortable in that place. Feel the temperature on your skin, the pleasure in the colors of nature. Appreciate the smell of the flowers or the trees, the music of the water, the songs of the birds, the peace in this moment.

Imagine yourself now standing up, surrounded by this beautiful environment. Your body is relaxed and your mind is free to welcome memories from your own life or stories that you have heard or read about women who empowered other women.

Let those memories come to you.

Now see two of these women at your back, each one holding one of your shoulders—one with her right hand, one with her left. Behind them there are two other women whom you are able to recognize, even if you have never met them. And behind them there are more and more women, each of whom has made a significant change in your personal history or in the history of women. You may or may not know these women personally, but you know their lives have influenced yours.

Now unite the strength of these women and their feminine energy with the wonderful imaginary environment you are in. Notice again its temperature on your skin, the colors and the fragrance of the place, the peace that it offers you. It is a safe place for you to return to whenever you might need it. It is your place in life, the one that you in turn can offer to other women.

Feel again the movement of your breathing and the sense of peacefulness created in your sense of womanhood. Feel its intensity and never forget it, as it is yours. It belongs to you and the women in your life.

When you are ready, stretch and take a few deep breaths. Open your eyes and come back to the room.

Reina of Your Own Envisioned Future

We have a responsibility to other women who came before us and helped carve out the path to our present opportunities. Our mothers and grandmothers, women in the United States, Latin America, Europe, and elsewhere who participated in the feminist movement, and others who laid the groundwork for Latinas and women of all backgrounds to be able to fulfill their potential. Using our seven strengths and all the other personal resources we can draw upon to reach for our dreams and goals is what these women hoped we would do—and we can't let them down. Ultimately, becoming *la reina* you were meant to be is about feeling that you're worthy of owning and fulfilling your own dreams. All the *reinas* to whom you have looked for inspiration now look to you to carry out their promise. Your future is their dream.

9

Sharing Your Power

Using our magazine as a forum to showcase the successes of
Latinas—so that our readers can read about a Latina congress-
woman or a Latina entrepreneur or a Latina actress—I feel like
we've empowered a lot of young women.
—Christy Haubegger, founder of
Latina magazine

It is important to discover ways to share our Latina Power so that it ex-
tends beyond ourselves to every Latina whose life we touch. Helping
our daughters and other Latinas to realize their dreams is what makes
Latina Power grow, and we can lend our support in a number of ways.
We can provide an inspiring role model for all of those with whom we
come into contact, whether they're our own daughters, other girls and
women in our family or community, friends, colleagues, or assistants.
We also can share our information and ideas. We can encourage and
mentor women who are starting out in the field of work we're already
engaged in. And we can take the time to guide our daughters and
nieces and neighborhood girls so they can explore who they are and
become whatever they wish to be, without the barriers encountered by
previous generations of women and Latinas.

What we've learned in our own lives is what we can teach best.
Being a successful Latina involves teaching our daughters to set goals,
to enjoy the process of learning, to face challenges, and to value their
accomplishments. We need to demonstrate to them that the old clichés
regarding what women can and can't become are obsolete. In this way

we can make sure that Latinas are free to create the future they envision for themselves.

Using the seven strengths to create a fulfilling and meaningful life for yourself is what Latina Power is all about. Sharing that power with other Latinas will not only be gratifying for you, it will enhance the well-being of our communities and our world. Guiding another Latina to develop her own Latina Power is one of the most valuable *regalo* you can bestow. The women whose stories are highlighted in this chapter reveal the many ways our personal power can transform lives.

Sharing the Power of Classical Music
Conductor Sonia Marie De León de Vega

In so many of the talented women I interviewed for this book there was a generosity of spirit that inspired them to give back to the communities they came from or to those who could benefit from their life experience. Having realized their own dreams — often beyond what they originally had envisioned — these successful Latinas wanted to help others dream theirs and turn them into real life.

Originally from San Antonio, Texas, Los Angeles conductor Sonia Marie De León de Vega comes from a long line of musicians — and dreamers. She pays homage to her parents and grandparents as the ones who ignited her passion for music and her determination to bring classical music to Latino communities. "My grandparents on both sides loved music," Sonia told me. "My father, Reynaldo Sánchez, was a guitarist and a trio singer. He had a beautiful voice. Sonia De León is my mother. She was very powerful in my life, my biggest influence. And I come from a family of very powerful, very strong women." Sonia's mother was a pianist, singer, composer, actress, and a producer of Hispanic events throughout the United States. She was the first producer to bring Hispanic artists to the Universal Amphitheater in Los Angeles, even though the entertainment business was totally dominated by men at the time. "But the message I got from my mother, my grandmother, and my great-grandmother—who was a candy maker and made delicious *dulces mexicanos!*—" Sonia recalled, "was that you could do anything, whatever you dream, but that you should be the best at whatever you do. Because my mother was a dreamer, I learned that I could dream too."

Sonia has been able to follow that dream, she says, because of her own determined personality, which is very much like her mother's. She told me about a pivotal incident when she was a ninth-grade music academy student that solidified her resolve to succeed. At the academy's annual awards ceremony a bright, blonde-haired girl named Kristin won Best Overall Student for the third consecutive year. Announcing the award, the principal stated, "The award again goes to Kristin, and I'm sure no one will beat her next year either." Hearing that pronouncement, a resolute Sonia told herself, "That's it—that's my challenge," and for the next three years she studied hard and won Best Overall Student as well as the best student in every subject for the following years until she graduated from high school.

Her educational experience wasn't entirely free from self-doubt, however. While finishing her bachelor's degree in music, Sonia realized she had put off taking the required class in conducting due to her insecurity about standing up in front of people and being in charge musically. But a very special teacher and mentor paved the way for Sonia's eventual conducting career. "I had been terrified about having to concentrate on the music while at the same time being aware of what all the musicians were doing," she explained. "David Buck was my first conducting teacher, and this happened to be the first time he had taught the beginning conducting class in quite some time. But he was so excellent—so nurturing. He saw talent in me and thought I was a natural. So he encouraged me to get into the master's program in conducting. He gave me a challenge, and I took it. From then on he became my mentor—someone who believed in me. And I still seek his advice, even today."

Sonia also was very much inspired by her father, who devoted his life to bringing the music he adored to the community he loved. She always knew she wanted to find a unique way to give back to her community as well, and of course her gift would be a musical one. After earning her graduate degree and spending about six years as a guest conductor with various orchestras and operas, Sonia was ready to deliver her *regalo* to the Latino community and the people of Los Angeles. She founded the Santa Cecilia Orchestra in Los Angeles, with the intent of reaching out to Latino children and families so that they could have the opportunity to embrace the classical music that is such a part of her.

Sonia's father had died just a few months earlier, and she chose the name "Santa Cecilia" in his honor, because he had been devoted to this saint, who is considered the patron saint of musicians. As she described her father's spiritual connection to Santa Cecilia it was clear how deep an influence he had been in Sonia's life: "My father always prayed to Santa Cecilia before singing and carried her prayer card as well as numerous paintings and statues of her. Every Santa Cecilia's Day he would gather all his musician colleagues together to meet at Saint Cecilia's Church in Los Angeles and sing *Las Mañanitas.* There were dozens of guitarists with beautiful voices who would show up, and ever since I was a child my father always included me. After they sang their songs I would play the piano. It was a wonderful celebration and tradition—one that he began in Texas and continued in L.A. In the last year of my father's life I took him on his first trip to Italy to visit the tomb of Saint Cecilia, where he sang to her a song called *De Colores.*' "

The performances of the sixty-two-person Santa Cecilia Orchestra, including the annual Opera Under the Stars concert, are one way in which Sonia shares her musical talents with the Latino community. Another is the musical outreach program Discovering Music, which involves the Los Angeles Unified School District and musicians from the orchestra. Because music education has been cut from so many schools, Sonia took it upon herself to give children throughout the Los Angeles area an opportunity to learn about and become inspired by music — on a very personal level. She designed a program in which musicians visit individual classrooms, so that they can have the closest possible relationship with students.

The first stage of the Discovering Music program involves a musician coming into the classroom and introducing him or herself by saying, "My name is [so and so] and I play [whatever instrument he/she plays]. I started playing music when I was [usually about five or six years old]." The musician tells the kids why he or she fell in love with music, how their career developed, and what it means to be a musician. Then they show the children their instrument and play something for them. A month later another musician comes to visit the classroom so that the children become familiar with two different instruments and are aware of two different life stories about how one becomes a musician. The third visit is a performance in the school auditorium by a group of orchestra musicians, and the fourth is held at a larger venue in the community, where the children finally hear the entire Santa Cecilia Orchestra. Friends and family also are invited, and the children can then explain to their parents what is happening, because many of these are families who probably have never had the chance to go to a concert. The children are excited not only to be able to share their knowledge with their parents but because they have met several of the musicians personally.

The approach to music appreciation that Sonia has developed is both unique and humanistic. Unlike the typical annual field trip to a huge auditorium where hundreds of children listen to music but have little or no contact with the musicians, Discovering Music begins with getting to know the people, the musicians. Then children become familiar with the instruments these people play, and finally they listen to the music that their new "friends" perform for them. In this way Sonia's program reaches out to youngsters with beautiful music that they may never have had the chance to hear. Children also have the opportunity to take music lessons, and one of Santa Cecilia's goals is to buy instruments for local students so that one day they can become part of their own community orchestras.

And how are children responding to this wonderful program? According to teachers and parents, students are deeply affected not only by the exposure to beautiful music but also by the musicians who have taken the time to share their stories and musical gifts. Sonia sends out questionnaires to the classrooms to assess the impact the program has had on the children, and she shared with me some of their reactions. One eight-year-old girl wrote, "When I heard you playing, I felt like everything bad in my life, and inside of me, went away and would never come back." An eight-year-old boy said, "When I heard you play I started to cry, because it touched my heart. And nothing has touched my heart before." And a nine-year-old boy who lives in a neighborhood overshadowed by gangs wrote, "I thought friends were the only important thing in my life, but I realize now that music is important too. And music can be in my life too." What greater benefit could you receive for your work than the knowledge that you helped to transform a child's life? The feedback from young people whose spirits have been touched by the wordless magic of music keeps Sonia focused on her mission.

That desire to share the power of music with Latino children and others in her community wasn't always so focused, however. It took shape as the result of an ugly incident that rattled Sonia's sense of justice. She was at a performance of *La Bohême* with her husband, and they were seated in the balcony: "I couldn't see the conductor, so I leaned forward. Two ladies sitting behind us complained that I was blocking their view. I apologized, but one of them said, 'You people don't belong here. You don't know anything about this kind of music.' Of course they didn't know that I was a conductor, but their attitude really got to me, and I realized I had to do something. That's when I decided to create my music education program. I wanted *my* people to belong there, and I told myself, 'I'm going to show these people who belongs here!' That incident was my Vitamin B shot for a lifetime!"

I was delighted to attend a performance of the Santa Cecilia Orchestra at the John Anson Ford Theater in Los Angeles. The lovely outdoor setting and sensitive rendering of pieces by Beethoven and Rodrigo made the evening a perfect marriage of music and nature. But the highlight for me was Sonia's masterful and passionate presence. We are so used to male conductors as the status quo that to sense Sonia's powerful feminine energy presiding over her musicians' interpretation of the classical works she had chosen was a uniquely thrilling experience. It was an evening I will never forget.

By acquainting Latino audiences with classical repertoire, inspiring Latino children, and nurturing young Latino musicians, Sonia Marie De León de Vega is fully engaged in sharing her musical talents as well as her Latina Power. If ever anyone truly belonged in a concert hall, it is this gifted and determined maestro!

Giving of Yourself as Others Have Given to You
Congresswoman Hilda Solís

One of the greatest motivations for using your Latina Power to empower others is a sense of gratefulness. When you have been encouraged and guided by people who graciously gave of themselves so that you could advance and flourish, you tend to want to do that for someone else when the time is right. Having been the recipient of genuine support, you take pleasure in supporting others. Hilda Solís, the first Latina elected to the California state senate and currently serving in the U.S. Congress, was the benefactor of such moral support.

Daughter of immigrant parents—her father is Mexican and her mother is Nicaraguan—Hilda was the middle child of seven, "Trying to get attention all the time." At the age of ten, when her mother had to return to work to earn needed income, Hilda took her household and child care responsibilities in stride. And she also assumed that she would go straight to work after completing high school in order to help out with family expenses. But a Mr. Sánchez—one of two important mentors in Hilda's life—pointed her in an unforeseen direction. "When I was in school, Latinos were discriminated against," Hilda told me. "They weren't advised to take an academic program but rather to prepare for a trade. So in my last year of high school, when our school counselor, Mr. Sánchez, came to me and asked about my plans for the future, I told him, 'I don't know. I think I'm going to do what my sister does—work as a secretary.' I was good at typing and didn't know about anything else then. Mr. Sánchez said, 'Well, your grades are pretty good. What about going to college?' And I said, 'Are you crazy? My parents don't have enough money to maintain the household—I have to work.' But Mr. Sánchez insisted, and he taught me how to apply for scholarships and financial aid. It was his tenacity that pushed me into college. Also, I was very rebellious and outspoken, and Mr. Sánchez taught me to use those traits in a positive way."

Hilda attended California State Polytechnic University, and while she was there she met the second important mentor in her life, Marisela Montes. Marisela was a young Latina working for an educational opportunity program, doing outreach and college recruitment. She hired Hilda to work for her, and as a result Hilda got a chance to go back to her old high school to recruit students for college. "I reunited with Mr. Sánchez, and the two of us were able to team up to enroll the largest number of Latinos ever to go to Cal Poly. Thanks to the help I received from both of these mentors—Marisela Montes and Mr. Sánchez—I followed through on part of the American dream, which I had never even been fully aware of. I finished college and later got my master's degree in public administration, and I eventually became a state senator and a congresswoman. Now I have become a mentor to others."

In fact, Hilda wasted no time in becoming a mentor to other Latinos. It didn't take long after Mr. Sánchez gave her the vision of college and beyond for Hilda to begin sharing her newfound power by passing along that vision to younger Latinos via her college recruitment efforts. And she continued to be involved in issues supporting opportunity and justice for Latinos and others whom the political system often neglects. When she was only twenty-one, she worked in the White House Office of Hispanic Affairs during the Carter administration, and later for the civil rights division of the Office of Management and Budget. Referring to his support of Hilda for U.S. Congress in 2000, labor leader Miguel Contreras said, "A lot of people thought that we needed not just . . . people who would vote the right way, but warriors in Washington." Her activist role in pushing for a higher minimum wage, domestic violence awareness and victims' rights, health care and education improvements, and environmental protection have earned Hilda the "warrior" title and won her the respect of constituents as well as progressives throughout the country. For example, she was the first woman awarded the John F. Kennedy Profile in Courage Award for her pioneering work in helping to improve the environment in low-income and minority communities.

Central to Hilda's political agenda is making sure that everyone — even those who barely are aware of its existence in their own lives — gets a chance to share in the American dream. "In my political career, my goals are to open doors for others, to create opportunities for people who have not traditionally been provided them," she says. "We are in a nonstop evolutionary process, and my objective is to be involved in making needed changes in communities like the one I grew up in. It's interesting, because when I go out into the community, older Latinos tell me that when they see successful Latina politicians, they find us refreshing. They're grateful that we see the broader picture, that we aren't simply driven by selfish motives."

Driven by her belief in justice and equal rights — and by the desire to give to others the opportunities that were given to her — Hilda's motives are anything but selfish.

Offering Latinas a Self-Affirming Mirror
Latina Magazine Founder Christy Haubegger

Younger Latinas may take for granted the growing number of Latino-oriented publications that have arisen in the last ten years or so. But many of us remember all too well feeling like outsiders at newsstands throughout the United States, rarely if ever finding ourselves reflected in mainstream magazines. Neither the subject matter nor the images we came across related specifically to our experience or our culture. Christy Haubegger changed all that, and her contribution to Latina culture has been a groundbreaking and empowering one. As founder of *Latina* magazine she decided to share her power by giving readers not only positive Latina role models but also a journalistic mirror through which they can see themselves in a self-affirming light.

Christy's path toward becoming one of our most influential and inspirational Latina entrepreneurs was set early in her life. Mexican-American by birth but adopted by Anglo parents, she acknowledges that the love and support she received at home laid the foundation for her confident, entrepreneurial spirit. "My parents never pushed me or told me I had to be successful," she says. "In fact, I think their idea of a successful child is someone who is full of love and who is generous and a good person. But when I was growing up, they constantly affirmed me. They told me I was beautiful and capable and strong and smart. They used to tell me all the time 'You can be anything you want—there should be no limitations on your dreams, no matter what the world tells you.' "

Christy says that her parents expected the world to tell her something different, because in Texas in the 1960s and 1970s the opportunities for Latinas were very restricted. Even though her parents are not Latinos, they saw that Latinos didn't have much of a chance, and they didn't want their daughter to be limited like that. Christy believes strongly that when parents lovingly affirm their children's strengths and potential "eventually you start believing it." And she did grow up believing in herself, confident that she could set goals—even far-reaching ones—and attain them. But she also realized that she didn't quite fit in, either with the mainstream Anglo world or with the world of Latinos whose parents looked like them. In fact, it was her non-Latino mother who lobbied for Christy to take Spanish in high school rather than French, which Christy preferred due to a "really cute boy" in the class: "My mother felt it was really important that I never be ashamed of who I am and that I be able to speak Spanish when people come up to me assuming that I speak it."

It was during college that Christy came to the conclusion that she was not going to fit into either a strictly Anglo or a strictly Latina world, but that she was going to fit into *both* of them. After getting her bachelor's degree in philosophy ("I knew I had to get a graduate degree, because nobody opens a philosophy store!") she decided to go on to law school as a way to prepare for doing something positive for the Latino community. "I thought maybe I would work at a legal aid clinic or with MALDEF [Mexican-American Legal Defense and Education Fund] or something, right? But I took a couple of business classes, got very interested in business, and I wrote a sort of miniature business plan for one of my classes. It was a proposal for a magazine geared strictly for Latinas."

This was just a few years after the 1990 census had come out and declared that the nineties was going to be "the decade of the Hispanic." It was a very big story, and it had caught Christy's eye. A Latina-oriented magazine seemed like a potentially viable business opportunity, which is why she drew up the plans for one for her class assignment. In response to her proposal the professor told her, "If this surge in the Hispanic population is really going on and no one else is publishing a magazine like this, you ought to think about doing it." Her response to him at the time was, "Oh no, I'm going to be a lawyer!"

As she got closer to graduation from law school, however, Christy couldn't get the magazine out of her mind. Having felt the absence of media images she could relate to as a teenager and a young woman, she knew other Latinas must be feeling that same lack. A Latina magazine was a compelling idea and a worthy project, but could she make it happen? Wondering whether she should abandon a legal career in favor of a high-risk proposition, she reasoned with herself before making a final decision: "Part of me thought, 'Well, sixty years from now, when I'm eighty-something years old, I would rather remember that I tried something big, even if I failed spectacularly, than wonder what would have happened if I had tried.' I also told myself, 'Well, maybe I'll try and start the magazine, because what's the worst thing that could happen? I could fail miserably and I'll be a lawyer—which is not so bad!' "

There was another important piece of her life experience informing Christy's decision to reach out to the Latina community with a new, inspiring magazine. During college she had signed up with a Big Brothers/Big Sisters program. What she learned from her relationship with her little sister changed the direction her life ultimately would take. Christy told me that she became a Big Sister for a young Mexican-American girl, and that their relationship was a turning point. "I saw how little her family and society expected from her, and I remember thinking, 'This is crazy. We are the same child, except that I got a very lucky break in some ways.' I believed that I could do anything I wanted. But her mother, who was a very good person, had been so defeated. And it hit me that 'but for the grace of God . . . ' It didn't seem right that my life should be so different from hers just because of where I was raised, that my dreams should be so much bigger than hers. It became very clear to me at that point in my life that the American dream is nowhere near fully realized for most people."

Thinking of the difference a magazine like *Latina* would make in the lives of girls like her little sister, Christy knew it was worth the risk. She wanted to prevent another generation of young women from being unable to imagine themselves as astronauts, business executives, or physicians, and she knew that a magazine where such Latinas told their stories could be crucial to girls like the one who looked up to her as a big sister.

It didn't happen overnight. Christy had to raise money from investors for whom this was a radical new undertaking, had to try and convince them that a Latina in her twenties had what it takes to build a viable magazine and a faithful readership. Again, she mentioned to me how important her parents had been in helping her get through that start-up process. "The reason I could even dream about starting a magazine," Christy said, "was because I had a family who told me I could do anything. Because of their belief in me, I'm very good at rejection—which is important, because lots and lots of people said 'no,' hundreds. . . . I try and learn from every rejection, so I ask people, 'What could I have done differently? What was the best thing I did, the worst thing I did?' "

Of course Christy did get the backing to launch *Latina*, and the rest is history. Without being in the least bit boastful, she acknowledges that in order to actualize her vision, she had to be a trailblazer of sorts. There were no other magazines geared toward a strictly Latina market, and thus no charted path for her to follow. She had to map out her own course—like so many other Latinas have had to do in their particular fields: "I think sometimes we make our own paths because there is no path already set for us. As Latinas we have to be pioneers. I think we're good at this because we don't expect anyone to hand us anything—because nobody does. We have to make our own trails."

Using her Latina Power to start a magazine that enthusiastically showcases the successes of Latinas from all walks of life, Christy Haubegger has given thousands of young women the sense that they too can become pioneers. And this is what sharing the power is all about.

A Creative Sharing of Faith
Singer/Songwriter Jaci Velásquez

Sometimes the process of empowering others takes the form of an artistic creation such as a novel, a film, or a song. While art always strives for an emotional impact, there are those rare books, movies, or songs that touch us in such a way that we come to view our selves or our world differently. When a songwriter communicates her insight in a compellingly artistic way, her listeners are given a unique gift. And this is what singer/songwriter Jaci Velásquez hopes her listeners receive.

In her early twenties, Jaci is already sharing her Latina Power with millions. Having begun her musical career at the age of fourteen singing with her family in Houston, Texas, she went on to become a stellar presence on the Christian music scene and now is a recording star in both the Spanish- and English-speaking markets. In the six years since she started recording, four out of her seven albums have gone gold and one went platinum. She has had sixteen songs reach number one on the *Billboard* charts. Aside from her musical talents, what Jaci brings to her audiences is a quality both deeply personal and spiritual. Her songs reflect her openness about who she really is, which is quite unusual in an environment where entertainers so often present a contrived image. Honesty, Jaci told me, is the foundation on which her relationship with her audience is built.

"To me it's really important to be honest in what I sing," she says, "because I think that when people try to put up a façade and become this artsy-fartsy kind of artist image, you can segregate your audience from you as a person. I want my audience to know who I am, because that's the only way I can relate to them."

One particular song that demonstrates her emotional candor is *"Cómo Se Cura una Herida"* ("How Do You Heal a Wound?") about the breakup of her parents' marriage, which had a devastating effect on Jaci at the time. Part of her *Mi Corazón* album (winner of the Female Pop Album of the Year at the Latin *Billboard* Awards), the song resonates with the thousands of listeners who are also children of divorce. "The song is part of a healing process—for me and for people who hear it," she explained. "So many people have come to me and said 'My parents went through a divorce, and I thought I was going to lose my mind. I want to thank you for doing that song because I really feel like God has used it to change my life in a good way.' My songs have been my therapy, so I am happy to be able to impart some hope and inspiration."

It is no secret that Jaci's source of hope and direction is her faith in God, and she values her creative ability to convey that belief through her songs. At a time when so many young people feel confused by conflicting life choices and bombarded by pressures and fears, the message of faith found in many of her lyrics is one that audiences find both inspiring and comforting. Given the harsh messages teenagers get from music, films, and advertising that push violence and heartless sex, Jaci's sincere, spiritual approach offers an alternative without sacrificing the sound or coming off preachy—peer power rather than pressure.

As open about her relationship with God as she is about falling in love, heartbreak, and the pain caused by her parents' split up, Jaci believes her songs reach out to young people looking for answers to life's biggest questions. "I think the new generation is looking for something, looking for some hope," she says. "And sometimes we get led off the path, thinking that we can find it in other things. We need people saying, 'You know what, I'm not gonna force you, but this is the only place you're going to find your inspiration.' Audiences are very open to that message. I don't ever try to preach or make others believe the way I believe. I just want to be a messenger of some hope, the hope that God brings into my life. When things aren't so perfect and life deals me a bad hand of cards, I just smile and know that I'm not going to fail. Because why would God allow me to fail? I know I can get through it."

Like many Latinas, Jaci's faith provides the foundation for her *aguantadora*'s determination to get through personal hardships. Combining that essential quality with her *espíritu creativo* and with the daring of an *atrevida* who is unafraid to bring an untrendy yet inspirational message to English- and Spanish-speaking audiences, this soulful pop singer shares her Latina Power through her honest, heartfelt songs.

Three Generations of Latina Power
Actress Angélica María

Known as *"La Novia de México,"* actress Angélica María is beloved in her country and throughout Latin America. She began her acting career at the age of five, but the story of how she developed her Latina Power and successfully passed it along to her daughter, Angélica Vale, began even earlier—with Angélica María's trailblazing mother, Angélica Ortiz Sandoval.

Growing up in Mexico at a time when women were not supposed to get a higher education, Angélica Ortiz Sandoval nonetheless studied business, then worked as a secretary, and went on to achieve things in the movie and theater industries that few women anywhere in the world were able to do in those days. Angélica speaks proudly of her mother's groundbreaking achievements: "She was a woman ahead of her time in this country—not only because she studied and had a successful career, but also because she divorced when she needed to do that. From being a secretary she became the most important producer in movies and in the theater—a real *vanguardista*. She was a very educated woman with a great sense of humor and a capacity for work that was unsurpassed. And she always believed in giving young people opportunities. She was an exceptional woman, but on top of everything she was a very humane woman, the best mother, the best grandmother, and the best friend."

Producer, writer, director, set and costume designer, and publicity manager, Angélica's mother set an example of an *aguantadora-atrevida extraordinaria;* she was determined to do whatever it took to realize her vision and was never afraid to take the risks needed to make that happen. When a door closed, she was already opening the next one.

Angélica opened the door to her own success when she was only five. She attended a children's party with her aunt and met the famous movie producer Gregorio Wallerstein, who was looking for a little boy for an upcoming movie. Angélica pulled her hair back and told him she would cut it to look like a boy. Wallerstein admired her determination and, after auditioning her, hired her for the part. That was 1950, and the movie was *Pecado* with Zully Moreno and Roberto Cañedo.

It's no mystery that Angélica inherited her mother's self-assuredness, as well as her theatrical aptitude. She went on to appear in twenty-one films as a child and thirty-five as an adolescent and adult. She has appeared as well in seventeen soap operas, one of the most popular of which was *Corazón Salvaje*. A singer as well as an actress, she has appeared in over 450 musical television programs in Mexico, Latin America, the United States, and Italy. Considered the creator of the *"rancheras baladas,"* she has recorded forty-five LPs and CDs. She also is credited with being the first singer in Mexico to sing a *canción de protesta*.

Angélica talked with me about how she has employed each of the seven Latina Power strengths in order to accomplish all that she has done: "Of course as an artist I had to use *espíritu creativo* to create a vision of my future—to write shows; select the movies, plays, and songs; and in some way anticipate what the public wants to see or listen to. I had to be an *aguantadora* in order to ignore the *chismes* that can be continuous and exaggerated—and to withstand the exhaustion of touring, the long hours, and the months when work might be scarce. As for being part of a *comadre* network, the only way I can conceive of work and success is by considering myself part of a team. One needs to be a *diplomática* to get along with some of the personalities in this business. And being an *atrevida* is essential—fears can only be eradicated with experience. After fifty-two years of experience, and I still see retirement far off in the distance, there is nothing that can stop me! Managing to become the *malabarista* and balance work and family was not always easy. But even though I had to sacrifice time for myself and with my family, due to important career considerations, I was able to have that balance later on.

"Do I feel like a *reina*? I certainly try to have that kind of strength.

When you have the example of a fighter like my mother, you do whatever you have to do to be strong."

Inheriting the potential for Latina Power from her strong mother, and then developing it throughout a lifetime, it was second nature for Angélica to encourage those qualities in her daughter, actress Angélica Vale. From the time she was born Angélica Vale accompanied her mother on all her tours. She even started working in the theater when she was only two-and-a-half years old. "We shared a stage," Angélica María says, "Happy together — actually the three of us! We were a team, my mother, my daughter, and myself."

What Angélica María communicated to her daughter, in words and by example, was to choose something that you want to pursue and then not to allow anything to stop you. Be prepared by getting the training that you need. And be well informed of what you are up against. Knowledge and experience, she told her daughter, will overcome your fears: "To be knowledgeable is to be strong. I have always tried to set an example for my daughter of a *luchadora*. I have tried to give her a model for hard work, tenacity, and being professional. She loves me intensely, as I love her."

Having been provided with an extraordinary model for a courageous, creative woman — her mother, Angélica Ortiz Sandoval — Angélica María found it natural to then model that behavior for her daughter, Angélica Vale. Three Angélicas, three outstanding women, and a celebrated example of sharing your power with those closest to home.

Fostering Latina Power in Your Own Backyard

Each of the stories in this chapter has brought to light various ways Latina Power can be shared. Sonia Marie De León de Vega inspires children in her community to take an active interest in classical music. Seeing her as the talented maestro, young Latinas with musical ambitions don't have to wonder if they could one day fit in to the world of classical music; with her as their passionate and powerful role model, they are assured that they could.

Congresswoman Hilda Solís is sharing her power by giving back not only to her community but also to the entire country. Her work in creating legislation that benefits minorities, poor people, victims of domestic violence, the environment, and more is an inspiration to all of us. She is proof that Latina Power can lead to political power, which, in the hands of women like Hilda, can create important changes in our society.

Christy Haubegger's founding of *Latina* magazine was a milestone in the development of Latina culture. Previously we had been marginalized by the media, but *Latina* created a presence for us. Seeing ourselves reflected on its pages affirms our identity and validates our aspirations. Christy's magazine continues to empower Latinas by publishing profiles of outstanding women in our community and articles that encourage readers to develop their potential.

Pop singer Jaci Velásquez shares her spiritual faith through her songs and provides young Latinas a role model who believes in putting her most deeply held values first. The young people who enjoy her music hear a message that encourages them to look for spiritual answers rather than simply following the dictates of a consumer-driven teen culture.

And Angélica María offers us an example of receiving the power from your mother and in turn sharing it with your own daughter, so that she grows up to be as confident, strong, and accomplished as you are. Her story serves as a metaphor for how each of us receives the seven qualities from other women—whether they are our own mothers or others who have inspired us—and then passes that power along to our daughters and other women in our community and elsewhere.

I believe that once we reach a point in our life when our own Latina Power is strongly developed, we each have a responsibility, an obligation, to share it with our communities and our world. We have been the recipients of wisdom, guidance, love, and support; other women have shared their power with us, enabling us to become who we are. Now it's our turn to give back.

How might you share your own Latina Power with your daughter, niece, neighbor, or other young Latinas? One thing that I believe in very strongly is paying attention to the individuals our children already are and validating their unique interests and passions. Many girls—even if they don't know exactly what they want to do with their lives—have a general sense of what excites them, what they're intrigued by, what gives their life meaning. But sometimes they have no idea how to create a path that will take them from a dream to a life in which they contribute to the world something they love to do. Sometimes they are told by family or society that they shouldn't follow their instincts and pursue a certain goal—because it's too unrealistic or difficult or inappropriate for a girl or a Latina. As role models, aunts, mothers, *comadres*, our job is to give permission to our girls to tell themselves that they *can* do it, that the challenge of life is to find a way to do what you love to do. When a young Latina has someone who cares about her enough to support her individuality and help her nurture her dreams, she is emboldened by that loving energy. And her chances of fulfilling those dreams are so much greater. We can provide that kind of energy to the girls in our community.

In addition to acknowledging and validating their dreams, we also need to be aware of the problems many young Latinas face today. According to a recent report by the National Coalition of Hispanic Health and Human Services Organizations (COSSMHO), Latina girls in the United States are "more likely than their non-Hispanic white or African American peers to face the four most serious threats to the health and education of girls today—depression, pregnancy, substance abuse, and delinquency." Contrary to certain popular stereotypes, the more a girl becomes acculturated to mainstream U.S. society, the more likely she is to fall prey to teen pregnancy, depression, drugs, and lower educational aspirations. It seems that recent immigrants, who bring with them (and whose parents bring with them) the desire for a better life and the determination to make that happen, are less likely to waste the opportunities this country provides. On the other hand, according to the most recent statistics, 23 percent of Latinas in the United States drop out of high school, as compared with 7 percent of non-Hispanic white women.

It is incumbent upon each of us to make sure our daughters take advantage of all that our society has to offer them—including the necessary education to realize their dreams. The first step is to make girls aware of their own creative and intellectual gifts, and then to help them see the potential for transforming those gifts into a fulfilling life—once they have received the education and experience they need. It would be a tragedy to see so much potential Latina Power wasted because there were too few mentors and *comadres* encouraging and guiding our young girls. So take the time to talk not only to your own daughter but also to girls throughout your community. Get together with other accomplished Latinas and forge a connection with a local school or girls' group. Tell the principal you want to visit on career day (or create your own career day) to tell girls about the work you enjoy doing—and how they also can take steps to do what they love to do.

I am also a strong believer in something that may sound a bit too simple, too obvious to even mention. But there is nothing more important in our daughters' lives than an inspiring example. Let me tell you a story about one of my clients. She came to me because her teenage daughter refused to attend school. We had a conversation about it, I gave her some suggestions, and she tried them with her daughter. But nothing worked. So my client gave up trying. However, she—the mother—decided to attend school herself. She took English as a second language and some computer classes. Because she didn't trust her thirteen-year-old daughter to be at home on her own while she was taking these night classes, she brought her with her. In the beginning the girl was rebellious and didn't want to accompany her mother, but her mom forced her. Eventually, the daughter began to realize that her mother was going to succeed. She was there when her mom received her certificate for completing the courses and when her teachers praised her for her good work. Those events had a real impact on the daughter. They inspired her to get involved in the process of learning and to take steps to improve her own life.

The *moraleja* of the story is that we can talk to our children, expect them to do things, encourage them, force them, bribe them, but there is nothing better than *showing* them with our own behavior. And the same goes for inspiring every woman, regardless of her age, who may need the boost our example can provide. Latina Power expands when we look to each other for inspiration and recognize our own potential in those women who generously reveal their power to us.

The Power Is Within You and Around You

I wrote this book for you because I know you have something valuable to offer the world. Like each woman who has shared her story with you in this book, you have the potential to accomplish what you dream of, and your Latina Power strengths can help you realize that beautiful promise. Latina Power isn't about changing who you are; it's about acknowledging and developing an inherited power you already have. You were bequeathed this power by the women around you — members of your family, extended family, and community — as well as your female ancestors. These women became *creativas, aguantadoras, comadres, diplomáticas, atrevidas, malabaristas,* and *reinas* because the cultural and political environments of which they were part demanded those qualities of them. As their cultural daughter you have inherited their courage, creativity, passionate determination, and skillful sense of balance. You carry within you their confidence, diplomacy, and connection to other women. All of this adds up to a collective wisdom that Latinas are fortunate to carry with them from generation to generation, and which we must now value and share generously with others.

My wish for you is that your Latina Power is manifest in whatever way makes you shine most radiantly. You are indeed the director, conductor, and *reina* of your own life!

Bibliography

The Americano Dream: How Latinos Can Achieve Success in Business and in Life, Lionel Sosa. Dutton/Penguin Putnam, New York, 1998.

La Chicana: The Mexican-American Woman, Alfredo Mirande and Evangelina Enriquez. University of Chicago Press, Chicago, 1979.

Creativity: Flow and the Psychology of Discovery and Invention, Mihaly Csikszentmihalyi. HarperPerennial, New York, 1996.

Digo Yo Como Mujer, Catalina D'Erzell, Olga Marta Peña Doria. Nuestra Cultura, Mexico, 2000.

Distant Neighbors: A Portrait of the Mexicans, Alan Riding. Vintage Books, New York, 1989.

Feminism on the Border: Chicana Gender Politics and Literature, Sonia Saldivar-Hull. University of California Press, Berkeley, 2000.

The Hero Within: Six Archetypes We Live By, Carol S. Pearson, Ph.D. Harper & Row, San Francisco, 1989.

Latinos: A Biography of the People, Earl Shorris. Avon Books, New York, 1992.

Medicine Women, Curanderas, and Women Doctors, Bobette Perrone, H. Henrietta Stockel, and Victoria Krueger. University of Oklahoma Press, Norman, Oklahoma, 1989.

The Millionth Circle: How to Change Ourselves and the World, Jean Shinoda Bolen, M.D. Conari Press, Berkeley, California, 1999.

Miriam's Daughters: Jewish Latin American Women Poets, Marjorie Agosin, editor. Sherman Asher Publishing, Santa Fe, New Mexico, 2001.

Moon, Sun, and Witches: Gender Ideologies and Class in Inca and Colonial Peru, Irene Silverblatt. Princeton University Press, Princeton, New Jersey, 1987.

Papal Sin: Structures of Deceit, Garry Wills. Image Books/Doubleday, New York, 2000.

Sacred Circles: A Guide to Creating Your Own Women's Spiritual Group, Robin Deen Carnes and Sally Craig. Harper, San Francisco, 1998.

Sor Juana, Octavio Paz. Belknap Press/Harvard University Press, Cambridge, Massachusetts, 1988.

Telling to Live: Latina Feminist Testimonios, Latina Feminist Group/Duke University Press, Durham and London, 2001.

Woman Who Glows in the Dark: A Curandera Reveals Traditional Aztec Secrets of Physical and Spiritual Health, Elena Avila, R.N., M.S.N., Jeremy P. Tarcher/Putnam, New York, 1999.

Women, Culture and Politics in Latin America, Emilie L. Bergman, et al. University of California Press, 1992.

Women in Praise of the Sacred: 43 Centuries of Spiritual Poetry by Women, Jane Hirshfield, editor. HarperPerennial, New York, 1994.

Acknowledgments

I would first like to acknowledge all the women throughout history who have made it possible for the women of today to be all we can be, contemporary women who are working to improve the lives of people in our communities, and our spiritual *comadres* who are always there when we need them.

A very special acknowledgment to our editor at Simon & Schuster, Marcela Landres, who passionately believed in this book, gave us her unending support and enthusiasm, and provided wise editorial guidance.

Grateful acknowledgment also goes to:

literary agents Angela Miller and Betsy Amster, for their graciousness and commitment;

Yolanda Hernandez, who tracked down our interviewees and made it happen, wholeheartedly lending her support;

Pepe Barreto, Miguel Weich, Aranzazu Flores, Ron Arias, Judy Lane, Jerry Velazco, and Marta Garcia, who enthusiastically helped me contact interviewees for the book;

my parents, who gave me the spirit of life;

my daughters, Eleonora, Gabriela, and Natalie; my granddaughter, Sophia; and my granddaughter-to-be, who are my deepest inspiration;

my sisters, Norma and Quela, who are always there for me;

the Latino men who have been supportive of what we Latinas want to do with our lives, with special gratitude to my husband, Alex, my soulmate, who is always so proud of everything I do and enjoys my success with me; my brother-in-law, Oscar, who always reminds me that to be truly powerful, women must also be financially wise; my brother, Bruno, who is the one I can forever count on, and who, like my husband, works so tirelessly against discrimination, racism and sexism; and my son-in-law, Brian, who also works for the same worthy causes as Bruno and Alex and is a great husband to my daughter and a wonderful father to my granddaughters.

And finally, my heartfelt thanks to all the interviewees who shared their stories and wisdom so that the readers of this book can proudly recognize and embody their own Latina Power.

Index